BLACK STARS
OF THE CIVIL RIGHTS
MOVEMENT

♦

Written by

JIM HASKINS
ELEANORA TATE
CLINTON COX
BRENDA WILKINSON

JIM HASKINS, GENERAL EDITOR

WILEY

John Wiley & Sons, Inc.

This book is printed on acid-free paper. ♾

Published by John Wiley & Sons, Inc., Hoboken, New Jersey
Published simultaneously in Canada

Design and production by Navta Associates, Inc.

For general information about our other products and services, please contact our Customer Care Department within the United States at (800) 762-2974, outside the United States at (317) 572-3993 or fax (317) 572-4002. For more information about Wiley products, visit our web site at www.wiley.com.

Wiley also publishes its books in a variety of electronic formats. Some content that appears in print may not be available in electronic books.

ISBN 0-471-22068-X

Printed in the United States of America

10 9 8 7 6 5 4 3 2 1

CONTENTS

ACKNOWLEDGMENTS

Thanks to Kathy Benson for her help.

INTRODUCTION

✦

In the twentieth century, African Americans advanced from semi-slavery to semi-equality in America. The term *semi,* which means partial or half, is used here because when the century began, black Americans were supposedly free but most were not much better off than they were during the time of slavery. When the century ended, many black Americans supposedly had equal rights but still did not enjoy the same opportunities as white Americans. Still, in the one hundred years between 1901 and 2001, incredible changes occurred in American society that improved the lives of and increased the options for African Americans.

Many of those changes came about as a result of actions by people who are are profiled in this book, including some whose names are familiar in civil rights history and others who are not usually associated with the struggle for equal rights. They were teachers, writers, inventors, doctors, musicians, men and women in the military, and businesspeople. Some excelled as individuals working alone and some made their mark as leaders of others. Some lived and made their major contributions to American life long before the civil rights laws of the 1960s truly established the legal equality of African Americans. Others were born after those laws were passed and never knew the time when the United States pretended that blacks were equal but insisted upon a "separate equality" that was a mask for discrimination. All resisted or overcame the barriers to equal rights and opportunities that could have blocked them. All are, in one way or another, "Black Stars" of the twentieth century. Taken together, the stories of their lives show that the twentieth century was not the era when legal equality was bestowed upon African Americans, but the era when African Americans seized equality for themselves.

PART ONE

✦

THE FORERUNNERS

BOOKER T.
WASHINGTON

(1856–1915)

◆

Booker Taliaferro Washington was born into slavery five years before the Civil War began. He was nine years old when the Civil War ended and slavery became illegal in the United States. He lived through Reconstruction, the post-Civil War period when federal troops occupied the states of the former Confederacy. During that time, black southerners enjoyed the rights to vote and hold office. However, once the federal troops left, white southerners quickly took away those civil rights. Washington lived his entire life in the South and experienced the frustration of being granted and then denied equal rights, so he decided that blacks should not demand social equality. Instead, they should work to achieve economic equality, and after that perhaps social equality would follow. He emphasized learning, but the learning of trades rather than book learning for its own sake.

Washington was born in Franklin County, Virginia, on April 5, 1856. His mother Jane was enslaved, and his father was a white man whom he never knew. When the Civil War ended, he was sent to work

in a salt mine by his stepfather, a man named Washington Ferguson, whom his mother married sometime after Booker was born. Between the ages of ten and twelve, Booker also worked in coal mines near his home in Malden, Virginia, as did many other children at the time. The work was hard and dangerous.

Eager to learn, Booker managed to obtain a little schooling before and after work. His mother also arranged for the teacher from the local black school to give him lessons at night. As he recalled years later, "[we were] a whole race trying to go to school. Few were too young, and none too old, to make the attempt to learn. As fast as any kind of teachers could be secured, not only were day-schools filled, but night-schools as well."[1]

One day while working in the coal mine, he heard two miners talking about "a great school for coloured people somewhere in Virginia." He recalled, "as they went on describing the school, it seemed to me that it must be the greatest place on earth."[2] The school was the Hampton Normal and Agricultural Institute (later Hampton Institute). In 1872, the eager sixteen-year-old began the 500-mile journey to the school, walking most of the way. He arrived with fifty cents in his pocket.

His decision to enroll in Hampton was probably the most important one of his life. The school's principal was General Samuel Chapman Armstrong, a man who had commanded black Union army soldiers in the Civil War. He quickly befriended Washington and arranged for a white northern philanthropist to pay the young man's tuition. Washington paid for his room and board by working as a janitor at the school.

Washington said he received two great benefits from his years as a student at Hampton—the friendship of Armstrong and the knowledge of the importance of vocational education: "labour, not alone for its financial value, but for labour's own sake and for the independence and self-reliance which the ability to do something which the world wants done brings."[3]

Washington graduated from Hampton in 1875 and returned home to Malden to teach. In 1879, he went back to Hampton to teach in a program for Native Americans, where he remained for two years.

In 1881, through the influence of General Armstrong, Washington was offered a position that would bring him worldwide fame: the principalship of a high school to train black teachers in Tuskegee, Alabama, that had been authorized by the Alabama legislature. The twenty-five-year-old Washington quickly accepted the offer. But when he arrived, he found that the legislature's $2,000 appropriation covered only salaries. There were no school buildings or land.

He recruited students from throughout the county, and held the institute's first classes in a shanty near the black Methodist church. The church was used as an assembly hall. Washington said the shanty was in such poor shape that "whenever it rained, one of the older students would very kindly leave his lessons to hold an umbrella over me."[4]

THE PRINCIPAL BUILDS HIS SCHOOL

A personal loan from the treasurer at Hampton Institute enabled Booker T. Washington to buy an abandoned plantation on the edge of Tuskegee, Alabama. The mansion on the plantation had been burned down, but he had the Tuskegee students repair a stable and a henhouse for use as classrooms. Black residents in the area contributed whatever money they could toward buying materials for a new building. One farmer who had no money, gave a "fine hog."

A white sawmill owner supplied the lumber, even though Washington could not pay him until much later. With this help, and money from several whites in the North, Washington put his thirty students to work erecting Tuskegee's first new building.

Tuskegee students gather for a history class in one of the many classrooms built with the skillful hands of students.

All of Tuskegee's buildings were constructed by the students. Washington was determined that they "would be taught to see not only utility in labour, but beauty and dignity."[5] By 1888, Tuskegee owned 540 acres of land, had an enrollment of over four hundred students, and offered courses in printing, cabinetmaking, carpentry, farming, cooking, sewing, and other vocational skills. In 1896, the young scientist George Washington Carver joined the faculty as director of agricultural research. Washington believed in practical, vocational education. Not only did it give people skills to make a living, but it also gave them independence and self-reliance.

Washington was not the first black educator to teach the virtues of self-reliance, though none did it more successfully. His name became a household word throughout the country, however, for another reason. In his "Atlanta Compromise" speech on September 18, 1895, at the opening of the Cotton States and International Exposition in Atlanta, Georgia, Washington urged black Americans to accept segregation and its second-class status.

He declared: "The wisest among my race understand that the agitation of questions of social equality is the extremest folly."[6]

The legendary educator Booker T. Washington poses with a group of Tuskegee Institute teachers and trustees.

Black members of the audience wept openly at this surrender of their dreams of equality, but the majority of white Americans loved the speech. White editorial writers and politicians took it upon themselves to proclaim Washington the new black leader (Frederick Douglass, the leading African American for decades, had died a few months before).

John D. Rockefeller, Andrew Carnegie, and other wealthy industrialists contributed money to Washington for black education. Presidents Theodore Roosevelt and William Howard Taft consulted him on which black Americans should receive governmental jobs. But Washington's critics charged that his opposition to nonvocational academic training for black people would keep African Americans on the bottom rungs of society's ladder.

Washington was a more complex man than some of his critics realized. Though he told black people to accept segregation, he also fought behind the scenes to end it. His work encouraging an investigation into black peonage (semi-slavery) in Alabama helped bring about a federal court ruling that the practice was unconstitutional.

In 1904, Washington secretly financed a legal challenge against Alabama for denying qualified black people the right to vote. He financed successful appeals in an Alabama case involving the exclusion of black people from a jury. He also helped challenge transportation laws requiring separate seating for blacks and whites. These actions were done so carefully that few black people, and almost no white people, knew about them.

In the latter years of his life, Washington was helped at the institute by its principal—his third wife, Margaret Murray Washington. They were married in 1893. Washington's first wife, Fannie M. Smith, had died in 1884 after two years of marriage. They had one daughter. In 1885, Washington had married a second time to Olivia A. Davidson, the assistant principal of Tuskegee. She died in 1889, leaving him two sons.

Washington passed away at Tuskegee from heart disease and overwork on November 14, 1915, at the age of fifty-nine. His funeral, which was held three days later in the Tuskegee Institute Chapel, was attended by almost 8,000 people. A special train bearing dignitaries came from New York City.

Booker Taliaferro Washington was buried in a brick tomb on a hilltop that overlooked the institute. Fittingly enough, the tomb was built by his students with bricks that they had made.

WHO IS RIGHT, BOOKER T. OR W. E. B.?

In *The Souls of Black Folk* the black scholar and leader W. E. B. Du Bois summed up his opinion of Washington and the passive path he urged blacks to follow in his famous "Atlanta Compromise" speech: "So far as Mr. Washington preaches Thrift, Patience, and Industrial Training for the masses, we must hold up his hands and strive with him. . . . But so far as Mr. Washington apologizes for injustice . . . and opposes the higher training and ambition of our brightest minds,—so far as he, the South, or the Nation, does this,—we must unceasingly and firmly oppose them."[7]

LIEUTENANT HENRY O.
FLIPPER

(1856–1940)

✦

Born in the same year as Booker T. Washington, Henry Ossian Flipper grew up to be the first African American to graduate from West Point, the United States Military Academy.

Flipper was born in slavery in Thomasville, Georgia. His mother, Isabella Buckhalter, was the slave of the Reverend Reuben H. Lucky. His father, Festus Flipper, a skilled shoemaker, belonged to Ephraim G. Ponder. Isabella and Festus had to get permission from their masters to marry and start a family. Henry was the firstborn of their five boys.

When the Civil War broke out, Ephraim Ponder, like many other Southern slave owners, decided to move his people to a safer place. He chose Atlanta. Festus Flipper arranged to purchase his wife and sons so they could all move to Atlanta with Ponder.

When the Civil War ended, the Flipper family, all free now, remained in Atlanta. Festus Flipper set up shop as a shoemaker. Henry and his brothers attended schools run by the American Missionary Association. One of Ponder's slaves had taught Henry how to read. He was an eager student, who later attended Atlanta University.

Recognizing Flipper's ability, James Crawford Freeman of Griffin, Georgia, a black man elected to the U.S. House of Representatives during Reconstruction, appointed him to West Point in 1873.

Flipper was not the first black cadet. Two other young black men had been appointed to West Point in 1870. Michael Howard had failed his courses. James Webster Smith, of South Carolina, also had difficulty keeping up with his academic work and had to repeat a year. Flipper roomed with Smith, who was eventually discharged from the academy.

Left alone, Flipper faced the daunting life of a black cadet at West Point. He did not complain. In fact, he stated that he was generally treated as a peer. He concentrated on his studies, learning Spanish and majoring in civil engineering. He too had "academic deficiencies" and graduated fiftieth in a class of seventy-six in June 1877. Nevertheless, as the first black graduate of West Point, he was hailed for his achievement by other blacks. It was a milestone.

In November 1880, Lieutenant Flipper was posted to Fort Davis in the Oklahoma Territory. At Fort Davis, Flipper oversaw the everyday, nonmilitary supplies that the men could purchase at the post exchange, the fort's general store.

The commanding officer of Fort Davis at the time was Colonel W. R. Shafter, who had commanded several all-black units in the Civil War, notably the Seventeenth United States Colored Infantry. Less than a year after Flipper's posting to Fort Davis, Colonel Shafter claimed Flipper had embezzled $3,971.77. He said Flipper had failed to mail this amount of money to the proper officer and that he, Shafter, had seen Flipper in town, on horseback, with saddlebags. Supposedly fearing that Flipper was about to leave town, Shafter had him arrested.

At the court-martial that followed, Flipper faced two charges. He offered an explanation of the deficit that was convincing enough to cause the officers to find him not guilty on the charge of embezzle-

THE BUFFALO SOLDIER

Second Lieutenant Henry O. Flipper was the first African American assigned to a command position in a black unit after the Civil War. In July 1866, while Flipper was at West Point, Congress had authorized the first peacetime units of African American soldiers. Legislation established two cavalry and four infantry regiments (later consolidated into two) of African Americans. The majority had served in all-black units during the Civil War. Mounted on horses, the Ninth and Tenth Cavalries rode on the frontier. The Cheyenne and Comanche Indians nicknamed them Buffalo Soldiers.

The cavalrymen of the Ninth and Tenth protected settlers from the Indians. They explored and mapped vast areas of frontier outposts. They also protected the crews of the ever-expanding railroads from Indians and outlaws. The Buffalo Soldiers consistently received some of the worst assignments that the army had to offer. They faced severe prejudice from the citizens of the postwar frontier towns. Nevertheless, they developed into two of the most distinguished fighting units in the army.

Flipper joined the Tenth Cavalry in Fort Sill in Oklahoma Territory. He later served at Fort Elliott and Fort Concho in Texas. He was involved in several fights with Apache, Comanche, and Kiowa Indians, on whose lands forts had been built.

ment. However, they did find him guilty of the second charge—conduct unbecoming an officer. This mysterious charge, never satisfactorily explained, was all the officers needed to dismiss him from service. The real story, according to some scholars, is that Flipper got into trouble by being a black officer who attempted to assert his social equality.

John M. Carroll, historian and author of the 1971 book *The Black Military Experience in the American West,* mentions a letter from a white officer at the post stating that the charges against Flipper had been trumped up. The charges were based not on any wrongdoing of

These Buffalo Soldiers, shown in Montana in 1894, served in the Tenth Cavalry. The Tenth spent twenty years in the Southwest during the Indian Wars.

Flipper's but on his daring to act as if he were a social equal to whites. That letter was subsequently destroyed in a fire, but even if it had been introduced at the court-martial, there is little likelihood that it would have swayed the judges.[1]

If Flipper hoped for justice by appealing to higher military authorities, he was disappointed. His dismissal was confirmed by President Chester A. Arthur and carried out on June 30, 1882.

Flipper remained in the Southwest. He put his studies of civil engineering and his knowledge of Spanish to good use, validating Spanish and Mexican land grants in the United States and translating the mining laws of Mexico into English. His translation of *Mexican Laws, Statutes* into English was an important contribution to international law. The National Geographic Society, the Archeological Institute of America, and the Arizona Society of Civil Engineers invited him to become a member. Clearly, they considered him a gentleman and a professional.

When the Spanish-American War broke out in 1898, Flipper sought the restoration of his officer's commission in the army.

Although Flipper had backing from several influential congressmen and newspapers, the army denied his request.

As the years passed, Flipper worked at several jobs: as an engineer for American mining companies in Mexico, as a translator for the Senate Committee on Foreign Relations, and as an assistant to the Secretary of the Interior.

In his retirement, Flipper lived with his brother, Bishop Joseph Flipper, in Atlanta. Bishop Flipper was an ordained minister in the African Methodist Episcopal Church. The other Flipper sons had done well, too. Festus Jr. was a wealthy farmer in Thomasville; Carl was a professor in Savannah; and E. H. earned his medical degree and became a physician in Jacksonville, Florida. But only Henry O. Flipper would go into the record books as a man who had cared deeply about the army and wanted to serve it, but was denied the right to serve even after repeated attempts to vindicate himself. He had to be content with publishing his version of the events in *Negro Frontiersman: The Western Memoirs of Henry O. Flipper.*

After Flipper died on May 3, 1940, at the age of eighty-four, his brother Joseph completed the death certificate. For "occupation," he wrote "Retired Army Officer." Years later, the court-martial sentence was reversed, and Lieutenant Flipper's remains were reburied with full honors in Arlington National Cemetery.

IDA B.
WELLS-BARNETT

(1862–1931)

✦

The Civil War in no way ended injustice toward African Americans. Blacks needed people to speak out and speak up for their rights. One of the most courageous voices was that of Ida B. Wells-Barnett, a crusading journalist and early feminist.

Ida, the eldest of Lizzie Bell and James Wells's eight children, was born in Holly Springs, Mississippi, just six months before President Lincoln issued the Emancipation Proclamation freeing all slaves in the Confederacy. Her parents rejoiced in their freedom. James Wells became a leader in the Freedmen's Bureau, an organization established by the government in 1865 to help former slaves build new lives. He and Lizzie Bell also helped set up a school for black children. Northern church missionaries, many of whom made great sacrifices entering the hostile atmosphere of the South, came to help. Ida was one of their first students.

All those positive experiences made Ida feel strong and confident. So she was prepared when tragedy struck. At age sixteen, Ida's childhood ended abruptly. Both her parents and her youngest brother died

in a yellow fever epidemic in 1878. Ida became responsible for her remaining siblings. After graduating from Rust, a high school and industrial school in Holly Springs, Mississippi, and passing the teacher's exam, she began a career as a teacher, earning $25 per month. She later moved to Memphis for a higher-paid position.

Wells somehow found time to attend classes at Fisk, a historically black college in Nashville, which led to another big change in her life. She discovered journalism. She wrote for the student newspaper. She also became editor of the *Evening Star* and the *Living Way*, two black church publications. The more jobs she had, the more money she could send home to her family.

Using the pen name Iola (from her friend Frances Harper's novel), Wells often wrote about race. She frequently got her subject matter from her own personal experiences. For example, she refused to sit in the Jim Crow car on a train in Tennessee. She sued the railroad company and won, but her case was later overturned by a Tennessee state court. She wrote about the railroad lawsuit in the church publications. She also wrote about the inequality between the public education of black children and that of white children in the South. By 1891, local white politicians learned that Wells was the writer behind these politically charged articles, and she was fired from her teaching position. Not to be silenced, Wells purchased part interest in a newspaper, the *Memphis Free Speech*. She became editor and eventually sole owner.

As African Americans struggled to establish their rightful place in America at the turn of the century, whites grew increasingly resentful. Lynching (or execution by mobs) became commonplace. So did envy of blacks who attempted to build decent housing for themselves and anger over blacks competing for jobs and establishing businesses. These were only some of the resentments that exploded into senseless assaults on black lives. In March 1892, three black businessmen were lynched in Tennessee for attempting to establish a grocery store that competed with one owned by a white merchant. Local papers asserted that the cause of the lynching was an assault by Negro men on white women. The outraged and brave Ida B. Wells dared to write in response: "Nobody in this [black] section believes [that] old threadbare lie."

Wells asserted instead that the lynchings were to discourage financial independence of blacks and the idea that white women could be interested in black men. These statements brought out a mob. Fortunately, she was away visiting Frances Harper at the time. Not only was the office of *Free Speech* destroyed, but Wells's partner, J. C. Fleming, was run out of town and Wells was warned not to return.

Establishing herself in New York, she continued her crusade against racial injustices in a newspaper, the *New York Age*, of which she later became editor and part owner. Publication of "A Red Record" (1895), one of many pamphlets she wrote, helped raise public awareness and action. The tone and writing style of "A Red Record" would be repeated years later in the speeches of civil rights advocates such as Dr. Martin Luther King Jr.

When blacks were barred from participation in the Chicago World's Fair, Wells joined Frederick Douglass and others in leading a protest campaign. She also began a campaign to have the word *Negro* capitalized in the press, pointing out that French, German, Dutch, Japanese, and other nouns designated for an ethnic group were always capitalized.

In 1895, she married Ferdinand Barnett, a Chicago lawyer and editor of the *Chicago Conservator*. The couple became partners in social action. Ida B. Wells-Barnett is reported to have crusaded with all four of her children when they were infants, nursing them along the way. A founding member of the National Association for the Advancement of Colored People (NAACP), in 1898 she presented to President William McKinley resolutions drafted against lynching. She organized one of the first African American suffrage groups, and in 1930, co-founded the National Association of Colored Women and the National

Afro-American Council. She also ran as an independent candidate for Illinois state senator. By the time of her death in Chicago on March 25, 1931, she was known nationally and internationally. Her autobiography, *Crusade for Justice*, edited by her daughter, Alfreda M. Duster, was published in 1970.

W. E. B.
DU BOIS

(1868–1963)

✦

Villiam Edward Burghardt (W. E. B.) Du Bois, one of the greatest scholars the world has ever known, is considered the founder of the modern African American civil rights movement.

Du Bois was born on February 23, 1868, in Great Barrington, Massachusetts. His father, Alfred Du Bois, died before Will was old enough to remember him. His mother, Mary Silvina Du Bois, had to struggle to make ends meet for herself and her son.

When she passed away in 1884, young Du Bois went to work in a local mill. He continued to attend Great Barrington High School, where he was the only black student, and graduated the same year his mother died. A few months later, the principal helped arrange a church scholarship for him to attend Fisk University in Nashville, Tennessee.

Du Bois arrived at Fisk in the fall of 1885, and he never forgot his first day there: "It was to me an extraordinary experience," he wrote. "I was thrilled to be for the first time among so many people of my own color or rather of such various and such extraordinary colors."[1]

During summer vacations, he taught black students in rural Tennessee. After three years at Fisk, he had gained a lot of insight into the depths and complexities of racism.

Du Bois graduated with a bachelor's degree from Fisk in 1888 and entered Harvard University as a junior. He graduated cum laude with a Bachelor of Arts in 1890 and earned a Master of Arts degree in history in 1891.

He studied at the University of Berlin in Germany for two years after graduating from Harvard. Europe was the first place he had ever lived without feeling race prejudice, and the experience had a profound effect upon him. "I ceased to hate or suspect people simply because they belonged to one race or color," he said.[2]

Over the next few years, Du Bois pursued an academic career that brought him nationwide attention. From 1895 to 1897, he taught English, Latin, Greek, and German at Wilberforce University. There he met and married Nina Gomer in 1896. The couple had two children: Burghardt Gomer, who died while still a baby, and Nina Yolande.

When his son died, Du Bois sat down and wrote what many have called the most searing essay in the history of race relations: "On the Passing of the First Born." It included this passage: "All that day and all that night there sat an awful gladness in my heart . . . and my soul whispers ever to me, saying, . . . 'not dead, but escaped, not bound, but free.' No bitter meanness now shall sicken his baby heart till it die a living death."[3]

In 1899, Du Bois's book *The Philadelphia Negro,* a survey he conducted of the social, racial, and economic conditions of black Philadelphians, was published. The book was the first in-depth study of an urban African American community. Today, it is still considered a significant work of its kind.

From 1897 to 1910, Du Bois taught history and economics at the old Atlanta University. During that time, he published fourteen studies on African Americans that were so important he could later say

WHAT ARE YOUR PLANS FOR THE FUTURE?

One night in 1893, alone in his small room in Berlin, Du Bois realized what he wanted to do with his life. "These are my plans," he wrote, "to make a name in science, to make a name in literature and thus to raise my race."[4]

Du Bois quickly made a name for himself. He received a Ph.D. degree in history from Harvard in 1895. He was the first African American to receive a doctorate from Harvard, and his Ph.D. dissertation, *The Supression of the African Slave Trade to the United States of America, 1638–1870*, was the first of nineteen books (both nonfiction and fiction) he would write.

truthfully: "Between 1896 and 1920 there was no study in America which did not depend in some degree upon the investigations made at Atlanta University."[5]

He had enjoyed friendly relations with Booker T. Washington for several years. In 1903, however, with the publication of *The Souls of Black Folk,* Du Bois posed a direct challenge to Washington's philosophy of compromising black equality.

In a period when the South averaged five lynchings of African Americans a day, when black southerners in rural areas were being reduced to a condition of semi-slavery, and when the Black Codes forced thousands of innocent black men, women, and children to work as unpaid labor on chain gangs and plantations, Du Bois declared: "We have no right to sit silently by while the inevitable seeds are sown for a harvest of disaster to our children, black and white."

Instead, he urged black Americans to unite with white Americans who believed in racial equality, and to use "force of every sort: moral persuasion, propaganda and . . . even physical resistance."[6]

Rather than concentrate on vocational training, he urged higher academic training for what he called the Talented Tenth (the top 10 percent) of black students, who could then go on to help teach, inspire, and lead the masses. He also practiced what he preached. In 1905, Du Bois was one of the founders of the Niagara Movement, a group of black professionals and intellectuals whose aims were to fight for full equality in every area of American life.

Booker T. Washington used his influence to try and destroy the new organization, but he failed. In 1909, the Niagara Movement merged with the National Association for the Advancement of Colored People (NAACP). Du Bois served as an officer in the new group.

In 1910, he left Atlanta University to join the NAACP in New York City as its director of publications and founder and editor of its magazine *The Crisis.*

In the pages of *The Crisis,* Du Bois supported American involvement in World War I. But after the war, the widespread lynchings and raw racism inflicted on African Americans led him to declare that all "of us fools fought a long, cruel, bloody, and unnecessary war, and we not only killed our boys—we killed Faith and Hope."[7]

While serving as the editor in chief of The Crisis *magazine, W. E. B. Du Bois started a new magazine just for children called* The Brownies' Book. *It was an entertaining and educational magazine to which children from all over the country could send their stories, poetry, and letters.*

James Weldon Johnson (1871–1938): Author of the National Negro Anthem

James Weldon Johnson, six years older than Du Bois, was the first black executive secretary of the NAACP. Born in Jacksonville, Florida, he was a talented poet. He attended Atlanta University, then returned to Jacksonville to serve as principal of a segregated elementary school. He briefly ran a newspaper, the *Daily American*, designed to educate Jacksonville's adult black community, and also studied law. He became the first African American to pass the bar exam in Florida. In 1900, he and his younger brother, musician J. Rosamond, wrote a special song to celebrate Abraham Lincoln's birthday, February 12, 1900. That song, "Lift Ev'ry Voice and Sing," became the unofficial Negro National Anthem.

Not long after they wrote the song, the brothers moved to New York City, where they formed a highly successful songwriting team. James joined the U.S. diplomatic corps and served as U.S. Consul in Venezuela and Nicaragua. In 1913, he left government service and later joined the NAACP, becoming its first black field secretary and serving as its executive director from 1920 through 1931. He led the organization in its support of major antilynching legislation in Congress and against all-white primary elections in the South. He resigned his post to devote his time to writing. He published several novels and books of poetry, and is today known more for his writing than for his civil rights work.

Johnson died on June 26, 1938, near his summer home in Wiscasset, Maine, when the car in which he was driving was struck by a train.

In 1919, Du Bois began trying to unite people of color throughout the world by organizing the First Pan-African Congress in Paris. In the years to come, he organized several more congresses: in Paris, Brussels, and London in 1921; in Lisbon and London in 1923; and in New York City in 1927. Although delegates attended from many parts of the world, the idea of Pan-Africanism did not develop a strong following until decades later.

The Great Depression of 1929–1941 led Du Bois to conclude that the NAACP needed to change drastically. In his view, racism existed because it was profitable to white Americans to exploit black Americans. Du Bois said that what was needed to fight racism was black economic power, even if it meant temporarily accepting racial segregation.

NAACP officials, who were committed to working for integration, were horrified at his ideas. In June 1934, they forced him to submit his resignation. Du Bois was now sixty-six years old, but he was about to embark on some of the most productive years of his life.

He returned to Atlanta University, where he taught for another ten years and produced two of his finest books: *Black Reconstruction in America: An Essay Toward a History of the Part Which Black Folk Played in the Attempt to Reconstruct Democracy in America, 1860–1880* (1935), and *Dusk of Dawn: An Essay Toward an Autobiography of a Race Concept* (1940). In 1944, he returned to the NAACP as director of special research. There he served as an associate counsel to the American delegation at the founding of the United Nations in 1945, speaking out strongly for independence for European colonies in Africa and Asia.

Du Bois also helped revive the Pan-African movement. He attended the Fifth Pan-African Congress in Manchester, England, in 1945, and presided over several sessions. Delegates from sixty countries and colonies elected him permanent chairman and president, and he was widely recognized as "the father" of Pan-Africanism.

In 1961, he and his second wife, Shirley Graham Du Bois, moved to Accra in newly independent Ghana, at the invitation of its first president, Kwame Nkrumah. Du Bois's first wife had died in 1950. He became a citizen of Ghana and settled down to work on a long-dreamed-of project: the *Encyclopedia Africana*.

On August 27, 1963, Du Bois passed away at the age of ninety-five. The government of Ghana honored him with a state funeral, and he was buried in Accra.

THE POWER OF THE PEN

For twenty-four years, through the power of his pen, Du Bois turned *The Crisis* into one of the most powerful publications the United States has ever known.

His NAACP colleagues would later say that the ideas Du Bois expressed in *The Crisis* "and in his books and essays transformed the Negro world as well as a large portion of the liberal white world. . . . He created, what never existed before, a Negro intelligentsia."[8]

Word of his death came to a small meeting of African Americans in Washington, D.C., on the eve of the March for Jobs and Freedom, where the Reverend Dr. Martin Luther King Jr. made his famous "I have a dream" speech. Author John O. Killens said someone told those at the meeting that "the old man" had died, and everyone knew without asking that "the old man" was Du Bois. For generations of African Americans, he was also, as Killens described him, "our patron saint, our teacher and our major prophet."[9]

His tremendous contributions to scholarship and the cause of human freedom were recognized by honorary degrees from Howard, Atlanta, Fisk, and Wilberforce Universities and several foreign universities.

CARTER G.
WOODSON

(1875–1950)

✦

Whereas Ida B. Wells-Barnett devoted her life to writing against injustice, Carter Godwin Woodson spent his life setting the historical record straight. He wrote about black achievement and founded Negro History Week (later changed to Black History Month).

Woodson was born on December 19, 1875, in New Canton, Virginia, to James and Anne Eliza Woodson. He was the oldest of nine children. His parents were so poor that all the children had to work to help the family survive.

Like Booker T. Washington, young Carter spent much of his youth working in the local coal mines. As a result, he was largely self-taught until he was seventeen. In 1892, Carter and his family moved to Huntington, Virginia, where he had hoped to attend all-black Douglass High School. But he had to work in the coal mines again and could not attend school full-time until 1895, when he was twenty years old.

Carter completed high school in a year and a half, and soon afterward was admitted to Berea College in Berea, Kentucky. Berea was one of the few predominantly white colleges in the country that

CARTER G. WOODSON

TEACHER, HISTORIAN, PUBLISHER

FROM 1903 TO 1906, DR. WOODSON WAS A SUPERVISOR OF SCHOOLS IN THE PHILIPPINES. HIS HEADQUARTERS WERE LOCATED NEAR THE SPOT WHERE THE FIRST JAPANESE FORCES LANDED AFTER PEARL HARBOR.

BORN OF EX-SLAVE PARENTS, YOUNG WOODSON COULD ONLY ATTEND SCHOOL ON RAINY DAYS, WHEN WORK ON THE FARM WAS IMPOSSIBLE. AT 17, HE WAS A MINER IN WEST VIRGINIA!

DR. WOODSON, THROUGH HIS SCHOLARLY WRITINGS, IS RESPONSIBLE, MORE THAN ANY OTHER SINGLE PERSON FOR FAMILIARIZING THE AMERICAN PUBLIC WITH THE CONTRIBUTION OF THE NEGRO TO WORLD HISTORY. HE IS THE ORIGINATOR OF NEGRO HISTORY WEEK, AND FOUNDER OF THE ASSOCIATION FOR THE STUDY OF NEGRO LIFE AND HISTORY. HIS WORKS ON NEGRO HISTORY ARE TO BE FOUND IN THE LIBRARIES OF EVERY IMPORTANT INSTITUTION OF LEARNING.

Alston for OWI

admitted black students, especially poor ones who had to work their way through school. Working as a school principal to support himself, Woodson maintained an average grade of 91 percent at Berea and graduated with a bachelor of letters degree in 1903. The year after Carter graduated, Kentucky passed a law prohibiting black students from attending Berea College.

Nothing could keep Carter Woodson from learning. From 1903 to 1906, he served as supervisor of schools in the Philippine Islands, which the United States had annexed after winning the Spanish-American War. He learned to speak Spanish fluently and took courses at the University of Chicago by correspondence while in the islands.

He then spent a year traveling and studying in North Africa, Asia, and Europe, including a semester at the University of Paris, where he became fluent in French. On returning to the United States, Woodson received a Bachelor of Arts degree from the University of Chicago on March 17, 1908, and a Master of Arts degree on August 28, 1908.

Woodson's enthusiasm for knowledge grew with each passing year. After a year of further study in history and political science at the Harvard School of Arts and Sciences, he moved to Washington, D.C. There he began the work in black history that made him famous— research at the Library of Congress for his doctoral dissertation, "The Disruption of Virginia." It earned him a Ph.D. in history from Harvard University in 1912.

From 1909 to 1918, Woodson taught at the M Street and Dunbar High Schools. In 1918–1919, he served as principal of Armstrong High School and was on the faculty of Miner Normal School in Washington, D.C.

It was a time of great turmoil for African Americans throughout the nation. In the nation's capital there were widespread efforts to make black Americans permanent second-class citizens. Woodson, like W. E. B. Du Bois and many other black educators, believed that ignorance of black history and accomplishments fueled much of this anti-black feeling.

Du Bois fought the ignorance with his writings in *The Crisis,* the magazine of the National Association for the Advancement of Colored People (NAACP), the civil rights organization he had helped found. Woodson saw the need for a history organization. On September 9, 1915, he and several other black men met in Chicago and founded the Association for the Study of Negro Life and History (ASNLH). Its purpose was to promote historical research about black people; find and preserve their historical records; publish books on African American history; and promote that history through schools, clubs, and churches.

In 1916, Woodson began editing the ASNLH's journal, *The Journal of Negro History.* In 1925, he organized the Associated Publishers, to issue books about African Americans that white publishers would not print.

For several years, Woodson had combined teaching with his other activities, serving as dean of Howard University's School of Liberal Arts and head of the graduate faculty in 1919 and 1920, and dean of the West Virginia Collegiate Institute (later West Virginia State College) in 1920–1922.

In 1922, however, he decided to retire from teaching to devote the rest of his life to writing about, editing, and popularizing black history. That same year, he published his book *The Negro in Our History,* which became the most widely used black history book in high schools, colleges, and universities for more than a decade.

Woodson would eventually write and edit more books on African American history than anyone before him. Some of his scholarly works are *The Education of the Negro Prior to 1861* (1915); *The Negro Wage-Earner* (1930), with Lorenzo Greene; and *The Mis-Education of the Negro* (1933). He started the *Negro History Bulletin* in 1937.

Among the books Woodson wrote for young people are *Negro Makers of History* (1928) for junior high school students; and *The Story of the Negro Retold* (1935) for high school students.

He was honored for his achievements with the NAACP's Spingarn Medal in 1926 and a Doctor of Laws degree from Virginia State University in 1941.

Carter Godwin Woodson died of a heart attack in his Washington home on April 3, 1950. He had never married. His life's work, declared African American historian John Hope Franklin, had been a "valiant attempt to force America to keep faith with herself, to remind her that truth is more praiseworthy than power, and that justice and equality, long the stated policy of this nation, should apply to all citizens and even to the writing of history."[1]

THE FATHER OF BLACK HISTORY MONTH

In order to reach larger numbers of people than those who read his journal, Woodson began Negro History Week in 1926. He knew that celebrating black history was important. "The hidden truths revealed at last to such large numbers," he wrote years later, "exposed the bias in textbooks, bared the prejudice of teachers, and compelled here and there an enrichment of the curricula by treating the Negro in history as we do the Hebrew, the Greek, the Latin, and the Teuton."[2]

Black History Month grew out of Woodson's Negro History Week.

MARY MCLEOD
BETHUNE

(1875–1955)

◆

Mary McLeod Bethune served for a time as president of Carter G. Woodson's Association for the Study of Negro Life and History (ASNLH). She was also an adviser to U.S. presidents and founder of Bethune-Cookman College in Daytona Beach, Florida.

Bethune was the seventeenth child born to Samuel and Patsy McLeod, both former slaves. Mary was the first of their children born free. Her parents owned five acres they had bought from her mother's former owner in Mayesville, South Carolina, where they grew rice and cotton. They also owned the cabin they lived in, having cut the trees and built the home with their own hands. On the day of Mary's birth, July 10, 1875, her mother "exulted, 'Thank God, Mary came under our own vine and fig tree.'"[1]

Young Mary became fired with the determination to learn when a white girl snatched a book from her hands. Black people could not read, the girl told her, and so the book was not meant for her. But despite Mary's desire to learn, "it was almost impossible for a Negro child, especially in the South, to get an education," she wrote

37

I WANT TO READ!

"Every morning I picked up a little pail of milk and bread, and walked five miles to school," Mary McLeod Bethune recalled, "[and] every afternoon, five miles home. But I walked always on winged feet."[2]

A new world opened up for her when she learned to read, especially verses from the Bible that told of God's love for all people. "With these words the scales fell from my eyes and the light came flooding in," she said. "My sense of inferiority, my fear of handicaps, dropped away."[3]

more than fifty years later. "There were hundreds of square miles, sometimes entire states, without a single Negro school. . . . Mr. Lincoln had told our race we were free, but mentally we were still enslaved."[4]

All that changed for Mary when a young black woman was sent by the Missionary Board of the Presbyterian Church to open a school for black children near Mayesville. With the support of her parents, Mary enrolled in the school.

When she had to stop going to school in order to help out on the farm, she said: "I used to kneel in the cotton fields and pray that the door of opportunity should be opened to me once more, so that I might give to others whatever I might attain."[5] With the help of scholarships from a Quaker woman in Colorado, Mary McLeod attended and graduated from Scotia Seminary in Concord, North Carolina, and Moody Bible Institute in Chicago, Illinois.

At age twenty, she began teaching at the Haines Normal and Industrial Institute in Augusta, Georgia, working closely with the school's founder, Lucy Laney. The school offered courses for black students from the elementary grades through high school. Laney, a black woman, convinced Mary McLeod that one of the greatest needs of African Americans was for dedicated teachers like herself.

McLeod next taught in Sumter, South Carolina, where she met and married Albertus Bethune in 1897. The couple had a son, and Mary stopped teaching "so that I could be all mother for one precious year. After that I got restless again to be back at my beloved work. . . ." Her husband died soon afterward, and in 1904 Mary McLeod Bethune moved to Daytona Beach with the dream of opening a school for black children.

She had only $1.50, but rented a shabby, four-room cottage by promising to pay $11 a month. She began making the rounds of black churches, where ministers allowed her to speak and take contributions.

On October 3, 1904, Bethune opened her school "with an enrollment of five little girls, aged from eight to twelve, whose parents paid me fifty cents' weekly tuition. My own child was the only boy in the school. Though I hadn't a penny left . . . I had faith in a living God, faith in myself, and a desire to serve."[6]

The next year, the school was chartered as the Daytona Normal and Industrial Institute for Negro Scholars. Lacking money to buy supplies, Bethune and the students burned logs, then used the splinters as pens. They obtained "ink" by mashing elderberries.

Within two years, the school had grown to several teachers, many volunteers, and 250 students. Bethune rented a large hall next to the cottage, using it as a combination classroom and dormitory for the students who boarded. She made mattresses out of corn sacks, and filled them with Spanish moss she picked from trees. At this time, Bethune began to concentrate more on the education of girls because they had fewer opportunities than boys.

Desperately needing room for a larger campus, she approached the owner of a local dump called "Hell's Hole." He agreed to sell her the land for $250, with $5 down. Bethune did not even have $5, but promised to return with it in a few days. She raised the money by selling ice cream and sweet-potato pies to black construction workers, and took the money to the owner wrapped in her small handkerchief. "That's how the Bethune-Cookman college campus started," she said.[7]

She wanted to construct a new building on the site, but again had no money. Mary Bethune pleaded with contractors for loads of free sand and used bricks, and promised workmen free sandwiches and free tuition for themselves and their children in exchange for a few hours' work in the evenings. In 1907, the building they erected was opened on the new campus, and Mary Bethune called it Faith Hall.

The black people of Daytona Beach and surrounding communities also gave all they could, even if it was just a nickel or a dime. Mary Bethune was a strong believer in interracial cooperation, and invited white visitors to attend Sunday services at the college. As a result, every Sunday some of the largest interracial crowds in the South worshiped on Mary Bethune's campus.

As the school expanded, Bethune said, "whenever I saw a need for

THE WEALTHY VISITOR

Mary McLeod Bethune scanned the local newspapers for names of prominent visitors from the North, and wrote letters inviting them to visit her. One of those who responded was James N. Gamble, owner of Procter & Gamble Enterprises. He arrived at the campus one day and was shocked by its shabby appearance and lack of buildings.

"Where is the school?" he asked.[8]

"It is in my mind and in my soul," Mary Bethune replied.[9]

Gamble gave her a check and agreed to become the school's first trustee. Other wealthy people also helped, including Thomas H. White, owner of White Sewing Machine Company. The trust fund White left enabled the school to build White Hall, its main assembly hall, in 1918.

some training or service we did not supply, I schemed to add it to our curriculum. Sometimes that took years."[10]

One day, one of her students became critically ill with appendicitis, but there was not a single hospital in Florida that would accept black patients. Bethune begged a white doctor to operate on the young woman, and he finally agreed. A few days later, however, when she visited the student, she "found my little girl segregated in a corner of the porch behind the kitchen. Even my toes clenched with rage."[11]

Within days, she had persuaded three friends to buy a small cottage behind Faith Hall, where she opened a two-bed hospital. It quickly grew to twenty beds, staffed by both black and white physicians and student nurses from the college. The McLeod Hospital served both students and African Americans throughout the state for twenty years, until Daytona Beach finally agreed to provide medical care for black people.

In 1922, the college merged with Cookman College for black men, to form Bethune-Cookman College. There were now fourteen modern buildings on a 32-acre campus with an enrollment of 600. Mary Bethune's work was supported by several black leaders, including Mary Church Terrell of the National Association of Negro Women and Booker T. Washington.

Her accomplishments as an educator opened many doors, and she used them to help African Americans throughout the nation. She was an adviser to Presidents Calvin Coolidge and Herbert Hoover. President Franklin D. Roosevelt invited her to the White House in 1934, and chose her to serve on the Advisory Committee of the National Youth Administration (NYA).

The next year, she was appointed director of the NYA's Division of Negro Affairs, making her one of the few African Americans with direct access to the president. Among her accomplishments as director were the securing of funds for Bethune-Cookman and other black colleges.

Always a strong believer in the power of coalitions to bring about change, Mary Bethune organized the National Council of Negro Women (NCNW) in 1935, which united several black women's associations.

She also helped found the "Black Cabinet" in 1936. The cabinet, made up of African Americans holding positions in the Roosevelt administration, lobbied for African Americans to be included in the programs of Roosevelt's New Deal.

In 1936, she was elected president of the ASNLH, which had been founded by Dr. Carter G. Woodson and several other black men in 1915.

Bethune received many honorary degrees and other awards in the decades since her "childish visions in the cotton fields," including the Spingarn Medal from the NAACP (1935), the Frances Drexel Award for Distinguished Service (1937), the Thomas Jefferson Award for outstanding leadership (1942), the Medal of Honor and Merit from the Republic of Haiti (1949), and the Star of Africa from the Republic of Liberia (1952).

In the Last Will and Testament that she wrote for black Americans, she said: "I leave you love; I leave you hope; I leave you a thirst for education. . . . I leave you a desire to live harmoniously with your fellow men; I leave you a responsibility to our young people."[12] Mary McLeod Bethune died in her Daytona Beach home on May 18, 1955, at the age of seventy-nine. Her funeral services were held in the Bethune-Cookman Auditorium and she was buried on the campus she loved so much.

MARCUS
GARVEY

(1887–1940)

✦

Like W. E. B. Du Bois, Marcus Garvey was a pan-Africanist. And like Booker T. Washington, he believed that blacks must achieve economic equality by depending on themselves, not on whites. Garvey tried to put those two ideas together.

Marcus Mosiah Garvey Jr. was born at St. Ann's Bay, Jamaica. His father was a mason, or stoneworker, and his mother was a domestic worker and farmer. Both were descendants of African slaves who had been brought to the West Indies by the British to labor on the sugar cane plantations and otherwise do the work of exploiting the natural resources of the islands.

Garvey was trained as a printer, and when he was old enough he traveled around Central America, editing and printing local newspapers. A keen observer of life, Garvey was troubled by the conditions of black life there. He saw the power exercised by the British and other colonialists. He saw what living under white control had done to the blacks, many of whom, unlike Garvey himself, were uneducated and unemployed and plagued by a strong color-consciousness that made

44

light-skinned West Indian Negroes discriminate against darker-skinned ones.

In 1912, when he was in his mid-twenties, Garvey moved to London, where he enrolled at Birkbeck College. He observed the ways of the British and took the opportunity during one Christmas vacation to visit several other European cities. In June 1914, after eighteen months in London, Garvey returned to Jamaica.

Not long afterward, he read *Up from Slavery*, the autobiography of Booker T. Washington, and was inspired by the conservative American black leader who believed that blacks bore the responsibility of "pulling themselves up by their own bootstraps." Suddenly, it all came together—the traveling and thinking he had done. Garvey recalled asking himself, Where is the black man's government? Where is his King and his kingdom? Where is his President, his ambassador, his country, his men of big affairs?" Answering his own questions, he admitted there were none. He then promised himself, "I will help to make them."

Shortly after his return to Jamaica, Garvey founded the Universal Negro Improvement Association (UNIA). He saw it as a vehicle for racial uplift and for the establishment of educational and industrial opportunities for blacks. Unable to inspire ordinary Jamaicans, Garvey relocated to the United States, settling in Harlem in 1916. He found a much more receptive audience there, where anti-black sentiment was at a historic peak. Garvey offered liberation from the psychological bondage of racial inferiority. He started a Harlem branch of the UNIA and soon had other branches in cities and towns across the country.

As the UNIA grew, Garvey structured it carefully so that every member could have a sense of belonging. Men could join the African Legion, women the Black Cross Nurses or the Universal Motor Corps, young people the UNIA Juvenile Division. He created important-sounding titles and uniforms and official UNIA slogans, prayers, poetry, and songs. He proclaimed himself "Provisional President of Africa" and dressed in a plumed tricorn hat and military regalia. Harlem photographer James Van Der Zee was hired as the official UNIA photographer to record the group's activities.

The majority of UNIA members were not the artists and intellectuals and performers of the Harlem Renaissance, but ordinary people—the people whites regarded as the underclass. Cooks, washerwomen, handymen, and mechanics responded to his message, to the chance to put on a handsome uniform and feel like somebody. By 1920, Garvey claimed one thousand branches in the United States, the Caribbean, and Central America.

Garvey believed that blacks would never enjoy equal opportunity in predominantly white societies or in areas under the control of whites. Instead of integration, he preached black separatism. His ultimate goal was to wrest control of Africa from European colonial powers, and to this end he advocated what became known as the Back-to-Africa movement. He urged blacks in the Western Hemisphere to return to their roots, to recolonize Africa and establish a pan-African empire. In the meantime, he was determined to promote worldwide commerce among black communities by establishing a shipping company that would transport manufactured goods, raw materials, and produce among black businesses in North America, the Caribbean, and Africa. With contributions from his thousands of followers, Garvey purchased a ship and sold stock in a shipping company called the Black Star Line.

This evidence of Garvey's determination to achieve his goals increased his popularity and the membership rolls of the UNIA. But it also disturbed many people. Other black leaders, such as W. E. B. Du Bois, were embarrassed by what they regarded as his buffoonery, by his posturing in military regalia. Those who were working to achieve integration believed that his talk of black separatism only impeded what little progress blacks had been making toward equality of opportunity.

Most whites regarded Garvey's movement with amusement. Some of the most racist applauded his separatist views. Government officials in the United States, the Caribbean, and Great Britain believed his activities threatened their national security. The UNIA's newspaper, *The Negro World,* was either called seditious or actually banned in Belize, Trinidad, British Guyana, and Jamaica. In the United States, the Bureau of Investigation (precursor of the FBI) began to investigate Garvey and the UNIA.

Garvey booked Madison Square Garden for the entire month of August 1931 for the first International Convention of the Negro People of the World. At the convention, the UNIA adopted the red, black, and green "nation flag" and adopted a Declaration of the Rights of the Negro Peoples of the World. The organization also elected officials for its provisional government and scheduled a parade in Harlem.

While Garvey was a master at organization, he lacked the business skills needed to make a go of his premier entrepreneurial venture, the Black Star Line. The company was plagued by mismanagement from the beginning. The UNIA paid too much money for old and rotting ships and did not acquire the necessary documents to enter the ports for which it was bound. When the enterprise failed, many of Garvey's followers lost their life savings. In the meantime, dissension was growing within the UNIA, and some of Garvey's most trusted allies were expelled. To add to his problems, Garvey was arrested and charged with mail fraud—selling stock in the Black Star Line through the mail when, it was charged, he knew it was not a legitimate business.

Deported back to Jamaica in 1927, Garvey never returned to the United States. He and Amy Jacques, whom he married in 1922 after divorcing Amy Ashwood, settled in Kingston where they had two sons. In 1935, Garvey moved to London, leaving his family behind. He died there in 1940. His widow carried on his struggle, on a much smaller scale.

Over the years, many people began to rethink Garvey's views and to see him less as a charlatan and a buffoon than as a visionary, and as a charismatic figure who established the largest black organization in history. He was regarded as especially ahead of his time in his pan-Africanist views. In 1964, twenty-four years after his death, his body was returned to Jamaica for reburial and he was declared Jamaica's first national hero.

A. PHILIP
RANDOLPH

(1889–1971)

✦

Like Marcus Garvey and Booker T. Washington before him, A. Philip Randolph believed that blacks should achieve economic equality and then social equality would follow. He spent his life working for that cause.

He was born Asa Philip Randolph in Crescent City, Florida, to James Randolph, an African Methodist Episcopal pastor, and his wife Elizabeth Robinson Randolph. He entered the world at a time when segregation—the next best thing to slavery, in the minds of many southern whites—was being firmly established in the South. To keep blacks "in their place," white supremacy groups were fast being formed, and such terrorist tactics as night riding and lynching were on the rise. As soon as he was able, Randolph fled the South. He was twenty-two years old when he and his best friend left their families and headed North to New York City.

Randolph enrolled at New York's City College and supported himself by working at various unskilled jobs. He soon decided that New Yorkers were not much different from southern whites in their

treatment of black menial workers. He rarely kept a job long and most times was fired for protesting his treatment or stirring up discontent among the other workers. His penchant for speaking up derived not only from the basic sense of dignity that his parents had instilled in him, but also from the ideas to which he was exposed at City College. Tuition was free to New Yorkers, and many immigrants took advantage of that opportunity. The sons, and a few of the daughters, of Jewish and Italian immigrants were also sensitive to the treatment of the working classes. The college was a hotbed of socialist ideas. Socialism favored collective or government control of the means of production and distribution of goods as more equitable to workers. It was radically different from the prevailing economic system in the United States and Europe, where a few individuals controlled production and distribution and the mass of workers enjoyed few rights. Soon, Randolph decided to help black workers better their condition.

He was able to do so full time thanks to his wife, Lucille Green, a former school teacher who had attended cosmetology school and opened her own beauty shop in Harlem. After Randolph married her in 1914, she supported them both while he devoted his time to his cause.

In 1917, Randolph and Chandler Owen, a good friend, began a labor newspaper called *The Messenger*, which they advertised as the "only radical Negro magazine in America." Its editorial stance was indeed radical. For example, *The Messenger* opposed black enlistment in the armed services during World War I, questioning why blacks should defend a country whose majority considered them "animals without human rights."

White labor unions denied membership to blacks, so the two friends tried to establish a black labor union. They also attempted to form black political organizations. Between 1917 and 1923, they tried six times to establish some sort of organization, always failing to attract membership and the necessary funds to continue. Their efforts did not go unnoticed, however, and when a group of New York-based sleeping car porters decided to organize a labor union, they approached Randolph and Owen for help.

Every previous attempt to organize the porters had failed miserably. The Pullman Company, which produced railway sleeping cars and hired the porters to staff them, took a hard line against labor unions and fired or severely punished any employee suspected of trying to organize one. After researching the background of the situation, Randolph agreed to help. He launched the Brotherhood of Sleeping Car Porters (BSCP) on August 25, 1925, at the Harlem Elk Lodge meeting hall. *The Messenger* became the union's official publication.

It took Randolph and the sleeping car porters many years to establish divisions of the union in major cities across the country, to rally the porters to the cause, and to gain the support of white labor. In 1931, the American Federation of Labor (AFL), a group of white unions, admitted the BSCP to its ranks. With the support of the AFL, the BSCP finally gained official recognition from the Pullman Company in 1934.

Five years earlier, in October 1929, the Stock Market had crashed, and by 1934 the country had slid into the Great Depression. Franklin Delano Roosevelt, elected president of the United States in 1932, introduced what he called a "New Deal" for Americans and successfully pushed through legislation that created jobs for many unemployed Americans. The event that actually ended the Great Depression, however, was the outbreak of World War II in Europe.

As the United States geared up to supply its European allies with war materials, Randolph was concerned that black workers would not get an equal share of jobs in the defense industries. He called for a March on Washington, D.C., as an effort to persuade Roosevelt to end discrimination in the war industries. In June 1941, as support for the march gained momentum around the country, Roosevelt issued an executive order banning such discrimination and establishing the Fair

Employment Practices Commission. In return, Randolph called off the march.

Over the next twenty years, Randolph and the BSCP remained active in organizing black laborers and in supporting the direct action civil rights movement which arose in the South in the mid-1950s. By the early 1960s, that movement was still strong, but its leadership had splintered. Randolph believed that the mainstream civil rights organizations had become too competitive in attracting media exposure and financial support. He called for them to cooperate in a major initiative to show the nation, and themselves, that they could work together. He revived the idea of a massive March on Washington for

BAYARD RUSTIN (1912–1987): BEHIND THE SCENES OF THE CIVIL RIGHTS MOVEMENT

Bayard Rustin was not well known to the general public, but he was a key player in the Civil Rights Movement and spent most of his life working for the cause. He helped found the Congress of Racial Equality (CORE) in Chicago in 1942 and participated in CORE's first Freedom Rides in 1947. He also helped Martin Luther King Jr. establish the Southern Christian Leadership Conference. Rustin was responsible for much of the thinking behind the Civil Rights Movement and one of the major architects of its nonviolent protest techniques. His greatest skill was in organizing and few would disagree that only a man with his organizational talent could have pulled off the March on Washington.

Rustin was gay at a time when American society was not as accepting of homosexuality as it is now. He could never have been a public leader in the civil rights cause. But he did not have the temperament for that kind of leadership anyway. He was a thinker and a planner. Referring to his great intellect, his companion and biographer Walter Naegle called him an American Socrates.

Jobs and Freedom—an integrated march, unlike the one he had planned in the early 1940s.

Perhaps taking a cue from history, President John F. Kennedy introduced a strong civil rights bill; but unlike twenty years earlier, his action did not cause Randolph to call off the march. He believed that the march would pressure Congress to pass the Kennedy bill. Plans for the march went forward, with Randolph's hand-picked deputy, Bayard Rustin, as the lead organizer.

On Wednesday, August 28, 1963, several hundred thousand Americans—of all races and religions—converged on the Great Mall in Washington, D.C., to call for equal rights for black Americans. They heard rousing speeches delivered on the steps of the Lincoln Memorial by the major civil rights leaders, including the famous "I have a dream" speech by Martin Luther King Jr. The enthusiasm, determination, and peacefulness of the marchers was impressive. A. Philip Randolph had envisioned the march as a climax of the direct-action civil rights movement, and it was. Never again would so many people be of such like mind and so determined to demonstrate peacefully for what they believed. It was the crowning achievement for Randolph, who at age seventy-four was considered the grand old man of the civil rights movement.

Randolph lived another sixteen years, to the age of ninety, and saw the passage of major federal legislation that ended legal discrimination and segregation.

PAUL
ROBESON
(1898–1976)

✦

Like A. Philip Randolph, Paul Robeson was a towering presence in civil rights history. He was born on April 9, 1898, in Princeton, New Jersey, the youngest child of the Reverend William and Maria Bustill Robeson. Both came from freedom-loving, strong black families.

Paul's father had been a slave. At age fifteen, William Robeson ran away from a Raleigh, North Carolina, area plantation and joined the Union army. He learned to read and write, moved to Princeton, New Jersey, and married. Maria Robeson, a schoolteacher who came from a family of Quakers and abolitionists, died when Paul was a child.

Young Paul adored his father and admired the "rock-like strength and dignity of his character."[1] Through his father's example, Paul learned to be loyal to his convictions, no matter what. In his father's church, he also learned the old Negro spirituals and hymns.

Paul grew up to be a stunning 6 feet 3 inches tall. He went to Rutgers University, where he excelled in his studies and was an All-American football player. As valedictorian of his class, Robeson spoke on equality for black people at his graduation in 1919. Paul entered

Columbia Law School the following year, and in 1921 married an equally strong-willed woman named Eslanda Cardozo Goode, a descendant of Francis Cardozo, a former enslaved man who became an educator and South Carolina secretary of state.

Eslanda Robeson encouraged Paul's talent as a performer. At her suggestion, he took the part of Simon, Jesus Christ's cross bearer, in a Harlem YMCA production of *Simon, the Cyrenian* in 1920. This brought his talents to the attention of playwright Eugene O'Neill.

Robeson graduated from Columbia Law School in 1923. While working at a law firm, he became furious when a white secretary there refused to take dictation from him. He quit the firm and never practiced law again.

Encouraged by favorable responses to his performance in a number of productions, Paul accepted the leading roles in Eugene O'Neill's plays *All God's Chillun Got Wings* and *The Emperor Jones* in 1924. The next year, he teamed up with pianist Lawrence Brown and performed the first solo concert of African American spirituals on stage in New York. The concert launched his singing career. He gave concerts abroad, and recorded his first album. He returned to New York and played the character Crown in the 1928 musical play *Porgy*. He also played the role of Jim in Jerome Kern's *Show Boat* in London.

Robeson's compelling performance of the song "Ol' Man River" in *Show Boat* was so memorable that it became one of his signature songs, along with "Deep River" by black songwriter Harry T. Burleigh. Robeson's favorite role, and the one he is most remembered for, was the Moor in Shakespeare's *Othello*, which he first performed in London in 1930.

Robeson, who was fluent in nine languages, made over 300 recordings. He also appeared in numerous movies. His first was Oscar Micheaux's *Body and Soul*, then the film versions of *The Emperor Jones*, *King Solomon's Mines*, and *Showboat*.

Throughout his many successes, Paul Robeson constantly fought against racism. He spoke out publicly against lynchings, segregation, poor housing, economic injustice, police brutality, other racist woes, and fascism. He approved of liberation for colonized African countries, and supported labor unions during the anti-union years of the 1930s.

Because of his outspoken beliefs, the U.S. government believed he was a member of the Communist Party. In 1941, the FBI began watching him. In 1943, they declared that he was a leading Communist. That same year, he became the first African American to play the role of Othello on Broadway with a white cast.

Despite the government's harassment, Robeson continued to hold fast to his beliefs, just as he had learned from his father. He later wrote in his autobiography, *Here I Stand,* "I saw no reason why my convictions should change with the weather. I was not raised that way, and neither the promise of gain nor the threat of loss has ever moved me from my firm convictions."[2]

Robeson's career suffered because he spoke out against injustice when he saw it. During a World Peace Congress in Paris in 1949, he said, "It is unthinkable that American Negroes will go to war on behalf of those who have oppressed us for generations against a country [the Soviet Union] which in one generation has raised our people to the full dignity of mankind."[3]

Cities and towns across the United States and veterans groups refused to let him sing in their halls. He nearly lost his life in Peekskill, New York, when a riot broke out during his concert. By 1951, in the midst of the Cold War between the United States and the Soviet Union, the U.S. government, the NAACP's Roy Wilkins, many other prominent African Americans, and even American television networks denounced Robeson for his views. The criticisms increased when he received a $25,000 Stalin Peace Prize from the Soviet Union in 1952. It was just one of many tributes and awards he received throughout his life, including the NAACP's prestigious Spingarn Medal.

Robeson as the Moor in Shakespeare's Othello, *his favorite and most memorable role.*

But even though his passport was revoked in 1950 and his travel abroad was restricted, and despite having his life threatened and being repeatedly called to renounce communism before the U.S. House Un-American Activities Committee, Robeson sang wherever he could. He continued speaking out against racial and economic injustice. When record companies refused to record him, Robeson and his son, Paul Jr., founded Othello Recording Company and recorded the albums *Paul Robeson Sings* and *Solid Rock.* From time to time, he even sang by telephone to assembled audiences in England and Wales.

Like his iron-willed father, Robeson remained unbossed and unbowed to the end. In 1958, he regained his passport as a result of a related U.S. Supreme Court ruling. After the court victory, Robeson sang to a sold-out crowd at Carnegie Hall, published his autobiography, and once again began singing and touring around the world. After Eslanda Robeson's death in 1965, Robeson settled in Philadelphia with his sister, Mrs. Marian Forsythe. On his seventy-fifth birthday, he was honored and his work celebrated at Carnegie Hall. He died on January 23, 1976, in Philadelphia.

In 1998, on the one-hundredth anniversary of his birth, fans and historians around the world celebrated his achievements. He also received posthumously a Grammy Lifetime Achievement Award.

PART TWO

MODERN TIMES

LOUIS "SATCHMO"
ARMSTRONG

(1901–1971)

✦

Louis Armstrong liked to say that July 4, 1900, was his birth date. Saying so was his way of emphasizing that he was a "true blue American." He enjoyed great acclaim in the United States and around the world and became known as an ambassador for that unique American music, jazz. As such, in his own way, he advanced the cause of black civil rights. He also did not shy away from criticizing segregation and used his fame to try to bring about change.

Louis Armstrong was actually born in New Orleans, Louisiana, on August 4, 1901,[1] to Maryann Armstrong, a domestic worker, and Willie Armstrong, a turpentine factory worker. They lived in a crowded part of New Orleans called James Alley in the Back o' Town section with Willie Armstrong's mother, Mrs. Josephine Armstrong. When young Louis's parents separated, his grandmother raised him. She taught him right from wrong and took him to church, where he learned to sing. When describing himself as a child, Armstrong would often say, "I stayed in my place, I respected everybody and I was never rude or sassy."[2]

From time to time during his early childhood, Louis also lived with his mother, new baby sister, and several stepfathers. The family was very poor, and Louis sold newspapers, sang in quartets on street corners for change from pimps, prostitutes, and musicians, and occasionally even gambled for pennies with his friends.

On New Year's Eve when Louis was twelve or thirteen, he took his stepfather Slim's gun out of the house and shot it several times in the air to celebrate the New Year. He was arrested, spent a miserable night in jail, and ended up at the Colored Waifs Home for Boys, where he learned discipline, stability, and how to play the bugle and the cornet. He left a year later, "proud of the days I spent at the Colored Waifs Home for Boys."[3]

When Louis was seventeen, he formed his own six-man orchestra. When they played, they swore they sounded as good as jazzmen Joe "King" Oliver and Edward "Kid" Ory, the two hottest bandleaders in New Orleans at the time. Oliver became Louis's mentor (Armstrong called Oliver his "fairy godfather") and even gave the teenager one of his own cornets. In 1922, Armstrong moved to Chicago, where Oliver had relocated, and played second cornet in Oliver's band. He then moved to New York, where he played in Fletcher Henderson's band. Henderson suggested that he switch to the trumpet, and he did. Louis stayed with that instrument the rest of his life. His cheeks expanded so much from blowing the horn that he got the nickname "Satchmo," short for "Satchel Mouth."

By the mid-1920s, jazz's popularity soared as a result of the development of records and radio. Armstrong's *Heebie Jeebies* album, released in 1926 by Okeh Records, introduced his unique scat singing style to the public. Although Armstrong wrote original music, he was mostly featured with big bands. He also wrote "I Wish I Could Shimmy Like My Sister Kate," but wasn't credited or paid for it.

A colorful speaker and a prolific writer with an engaging sense of humor, Louis often called his associates "Pops" and signed his letters "Red beans and ricely yours," a reference to his favorite meal.

As his popularity soared, Armstrong was in a position to do what few other blacks could in the 1940s and 50s. He told an interviewer in 1967, "I had it put in my contracts that I wouldn't play no place I couldn't stay. I was the first Negro in the business to crack them big white hotels—Oh yeah! I pioneered, Pops! Nobody much remembers that these days."[4]

Armstrong broke down a number of racial barriers, especially as the first African American to play on stages that had previously been open only to white acts. In 1957, when nine black teenagers attempted to integrate Central High School in Little Rock, Arkansas, Governor Orval Faubus ordered state National Guard units to prevent them from doing so. Since Little Rock was under federal court order to admit black students to Central High, President Dwight D. Eisenhower had no choice but to send federal troops to Little Rock to enforce the court order. When he hesitated to do so, Louis Armstrong criticized him publicly and offered to personally go to Little Rock to escort the students to the school.

Louis Armstrong was known throughout the world. He appeared in some sixty movies, including *Pennies from Heaven* (1936) and *Hello Dolly* (1969). He toured Europe and Africa, and recorded thousands of songs individually and with other singers like Ella Fitzgerald and Billie Holiday. A role model for aspiring musicians, he won over two hundred awards, received honorary doctorates, and traveled as a cultural ambassador of goodwill for the U.S. State Department.

Armstrong died in his sleep at his home in Queens, New York, on July 6, 1971, after suffering a heart attack earlier that year. His home, now a city and national landmark, is the Louis Armstrong House and Archives run by Queens College, City University of New York. African nations have honored Louis Armstrong with postage stamps, and the United States issued a Louis Armstrong postage stamp in 1995.

Born into extreme poverty at the turn of the century, Louis Armstrong's life is proof that with determination, hope, hard work, common sense, and sacrifice, any young black boy or girl can one day become a star.

Armstrong's music lives on today. Moviegoers can hear him sing "What a Wonderful World" in the movie *Good Morning, Vietnam,* and "Talk to the Animals" in Eddie Murphy's film version of *Dr. Dolittle.*

Thurgood
MARSHALL

(1908–1993)

✦

Like Louis Armstrong, Thurgood Marshall was born into an America where discrimination was condoned, segregation was legal, lynchings were common, and the barriers between black and white seemed insurmountable. He became an attorney and spent most of his career fighting segregation in local, state, and federal courts. In 1967, he became the first African American justice on the U.S. Supreme Court, a position that enabled him to further influence the laws that affected African Americans.

Marshall was born and spent most of his childhood in Baltimore, Maryland. Both his parents had steady jobs; his father, William, worked as a railroad car porter, and his mother, Norma, taught school. Thurgood and his brother Aubrey were brought up to be proud of their heritage and of themselves and to be the best they could at whatever they did. The elder Marshalls hoped their sons would become doctors. Next to ministers, doctors were the most highly respected men in the black community. At the time, there were few black lawyers.

69

Marshall attended Lincoln University, a black college in Pennsylvania. At the end of his junior year, he married Vivien Burey, whom everyone called Buster, a student at the University of Pennsylvania who dropped out of school to live with her husband. He majored in pre-dentistry at Lincoln but decided to attend law school after graduation. As a youth, he had read the U.S. Constitution and wondered why its words did not seem to apply to blacks. His father had told him that the Constitution and its amendments were the way things were supposed to be, not the way they actually were, and some day that would change. Marshall was determined to use the Constitution and the courts to make things the way they were supposed to be.

There was no law school for blacks in Maryland, so Marshall applied to Howard University in Washington, D.C. He and Buster moved in with his parents to save money, and Buster worked to pay her husband's tuition. Eventually, they had two children.

Marshall was fortunate to attend Howard University Law School at the time when the school was making the reorganization of its law school a top priority. Charles Hamilton Houston headed the law school and also taught courses: most important, a series of seminars on how existing laws could be made to work for black people. In his sophomore year, Marshall took a course on civil rights law with Houston, the first time such a course had ever been taught.

After obtaining his law degree, Marshall tried to set up a practice in Baltimore. But he soon grew bored with divorce and property cases. Charles Hamilton Houston left Howard to become the chief counsel for the National Association for the Advancement of Colored People (NAACP), and he asked Marshall to assist him in a case involving the denial of admission of a black man to the University of Maryland Law School. Marshall worked with Houston, and in the end the Maryland Court of Appeals ruled that the state of Maryland must either pay full tuition and commuting expenses to an out-of-state law school or set up a law school for blacks.

Shortly after that, Houston invited Marshall to join him at NAACP headquarters in New York City. Marshall and Buster moved North, and Marshall began an exciting and sometimes dangerous career as a counsel for the civil rights organization. He tried to be everywhere at once: a school desegregation case here, an unequal pay case there, a lynching case somewhere else. Occasionally, he risked his life by going to small towns in the Deep South to represent blacks accused of major crimes. He rarely succeeded against a system controlled by whites and in which blacks were not allowed to serve on juries, but he was determined to at least put up a good fight.

Marshall successfully argued a variety of cases, such as one concerning voting rights in Texas and another about segregation on interstate buses in Virginia. In 1940, he won the first of twenty-nine cases he argued before the U.S. Supreme Court. Gradually, however, he and others who set policy at the NAACP decided that with his limited staff and financial resources he had to concentrate on cases in which the law seemed to be on the side of black people and that he had a chance of winning. Eventually, they settled on school desegregation.

Back in 1895, in *Plessy v. Ferguson,* a public transportation case in Louisiana, the U.S. Supreme Court had ruled that "separate but equal" facilities for blacks and whites were constitutional, even though everyone knew that facilities just for blacks were never equal to those of whites. In 1945, in the face of glaring evidence that segregated schools for blacks were not equal to white schools, Marshall and the NAACP decided to launch a direct attack on segregation. They felt the time was right. Many black soldiers and pilots had distinguished themselves in World War II, which had just ended. Many whites, especially in the North, had come to feel that segregation was wrong. Some of them worried about the growing threat of Communism in the world and the charge, hard to dispute, by the Communist Soviet Union that the United States preached democracy but did not practice it. Over the course of ten years, Marshall and the NAACP pursued a carefully planned campaign to fight school segregation in the courts.

That campaign culminated in the case of *Brown v. Board of Education,* which was actually a group of four cases concerning school segregation in four different states. The case eventually made its way to the U.S. Supreme Court, where Marshall and his co-counsels successfully proved that segregated schools for blacks not only were not equal to those for whites but were also detrimental to the educational and psychological well-being of their students. "Equal," Marshall stated to the nine justices of the Court, "means getting the *same* thing, at the *same* time and in the *same* place."[1]

Marshall successfully argued his case. In a landmark decision handed down in May 1954, the Court ruled that separate but equal education was unconstitutional and opened the way for the end of legal segregation in all areas of American life. It would take many more years of court cases and two major pieces of federal legislation in the 1960s, but eventually the legal underpinnings of segregation were kicked out from under it.

Buster Marshall died of cancer in 1955. Not long after her death, Marshall met and married Cecilia Suyat, a staffer in the NAACP office. They had no children.

President John F. Kennedy, who assumed office in January 1961, appointed a large number of blacks to federal posts. Marshall served as a judge on the United States Court of Appeals for the Second Circuit, which covered New York, Connecticut, and Vermont. During his four-year tenure on that court, he handed down a total of 112 rulings, all of them later upheld by the Supreme Court. In 1965, President Lyndon B. Johnson, who succeeded to the presidency after Kennedy's assassination in 1963, named Marshall to the post of Solicitor General, effectively the government's chief appellate (or appeals) lawyer. In that position, he won fourteen of the nineteen cases he argued before the Supreme Court.

In 1967, when a vacancy occurred on the U.S. Supreme Court, Johnson appointed Marshall, who became the first black Associate Justice. He joined a fairly liberal Court. But over the years, as politically conservative presidents appointed like-minded judges to serve, Marshall often found himself in the minority on basic issues of rights. He became famous for his dissents, or official differences of opinion from the majority of the Justices. In one dissent from a conservative majority ruling, he declared that "[p]ower, not reason, is the new currency of this Court's decision making."[2]

Marshall retired from the Supreme Court in 1991 for reasons of ill health and died of heart failure in 1993 at the age of eighty-four. No single person had done more to influence civil rights legislation in this country in the twentieth century.

A D A M C L A Y T O N
POWELL Jr.

(1908–1972)

✦

Adam Clayton Powell Jr. was born in the same year as Thurgood Marshall and, like Marshall, achieved a status in the U.S. government that black Americans born in earlier times could only have dreamed about. Also like Marshall, he used that status to make life better for people of all colors.

Powell was born into a middle-class family and was well educated. His father, the Reverend Adam Clayton Powell Sr., was pastor of Immanuel Baptist Church in New Haven, Connecticut. Soon after the birth of his son, the Reverend Powell accepted an invitation to become pastor of the hundred-year-old Abyssinian Baptist Church in New York City.

Adam Jr. attended college at Colgate University, then did further study at Columbia University in New York City. He earned his degree in divinity from Shaw University in Raleigh, North Carolina, in 1934, then returned home to serve as business manager and director of Abyssinian's social and educational programs. The Great Depression had descended upon the United States, and black Americans were

especially hard hit. Seeing the misery around him in Harlem, Powell began to identify with poor blacks. In a time when the federal government had few social welfare programs, he organized and directed at Abyssinian the largest relief bureau ever established by African Americans.

Powell wrote a regular column for the *Amsterdam News*, New York's largest African American weekly newspaper, exposing the conditions of poverty, hunger, and discrimination for Harlemites and African Americans generally. He also led protests against various forms of discrimination against blacks. When in late 1937 his father retired and he assumed the pastorship of Abyssinian church, he had a major power base from which to work.

Powell ran for a seat on New York's City Council and was the first African American to sit on the council. Three years later, he ran for election to the U.S. House of Representatives and became the fourth black man to serve in that body since 1901. When he took his seat in the House in 1945, he automatically integrated such congressional facilities as the gymnasium and the barbershop and instructed his staff to use the congressional dining room whether they were hungry or not.

At the time, Washington, D.C., was as deeply segregated as any southern city, and Powell wasted no time introducing measures to end discrimination in public transportation and the practice of barring black journalists from the congressional galleries. It was clear that he intended to represent not just his constituents in Harlem but all African Americans. He was re-elected again and again.

By 1960, when President John F. Kennedy, a Democrat, won election and Democrats were in the majority in the House, Powell had enough seniority to qualify for the post of chairman of the House Education and Labor Committee. It was the most powerful position a black man had ever held in the federal government. Until 1969, when the Republican administration of President Richard M. Nixon came to office, Powell used his power to shepherd a number of important bills through the committee and to passage in Congress. Legislation for which he is credited includes increasing the federal minimum wage and extending it to more occupations, providing for the training of teachers of disabled children, establishing job training programs, increasing the number of children eligible for free school lunches, increasing federal assistance to public libraries, establishing the National Council on the Arts, the Older Americans Act of 1965, and much more. He was considered one of the major architects of the War on Poverty, started under President Kennedy and continued after Kennedy's assassination by President Lyndon B. Johnson. All this legislation benefited not just black people but poor people, workers, children, and the disabled of all races.

Powell's horizons extended beyond the borders of his own country. Like other black Americans—and like Du Bois and Garvey before him—he felt a growing bond with other nonwhite people of the world. He urged African Americans to work against apartheid, the official separation of the races, in white-ruled South Africa. He envisioned a political coalition between African Americans and Puerto Ricans on the mainland United States. After marrying his third wife (earlier marriages to pianist and singer Hazel Scott and actress Isabel Washington had ended in divorce), Yvette Diego Flores Diago, Powell commuted back and forth between Puerto Rico, where Yvette lived with their son; Harlem, where he continued to serve as pastor at Abyssinian Baptist Church; and Washington, D.C., where he sat in Congress.

Powell supported statehood for Puerto Rico and came under fire from Puerto Rican nationalists who were determined to have an independent country. After a group of nationalists attacked his villa in Puerto Rico, Powell arranged to go to Europe to study equal-employment opportunities for women. Two young, unmarried women from his Washington staff accompanied him, and according to press reports they spent far more time going to nightclubs and taking sightseeing cruises than studying employment. The trip created a furor back home and was characterized as a "shameless junket." Congress moved to censure him for misusing taxpayers' money. Powell countered that many other congressmen took such luxury trips and that racism and personal and political enmity against him were at the root of the censure.

As if he were not in enough trouble, Powell learned that the IRS was charging him with paying too little in income taxes for the years 1949–1955 (the second time the IRS had made this charge). Then there was the long-running legal battle with one Mrs. Esther James, whom he had accused in 1960 of collecting payoffs for the police in Harlem. She sued him in court and won. He refused to pay the damages assessed and in 1963 the New York Supreme Court issued a warrant for his arrest. After that, Powell returned to New York City only on Sundays to deliver his sermon at Abyssinian Baptist Church.

In one such sermon, delivered on May 29, 1966, he used the term "black power" and later claimed to have originated it. But the leader of the Student Nonviolent Coordinating Committee, Stokely Carmichael, who issued a call for "Black Power!" during a speech in June 1966, generally gets the credit. Nevertheless, Powell had sensed that the mood of black Americans was changing. They were tired of nonviolence and turning the other cheek and waiting for white people to give them equality. More and more, there was talk of seizing the rights they were due.

All of Powell's troubles seemed to converge. He was re-elected to Congress in 1966, but when he arrived at the House of Representatives for the start of the new congressional term on February 28, 1967, his fellow representatives refused to seat him, charging him with unbecoming conduct and misusing public funds. Two years later, the U.S. Supreme Court ruled that the House had acted unconstitutionally, pointing out that qualifications for admission to the House were age, citizenship, and state residence. Congress has the power to expel a member by a two-thirds vote, but it cannot bar a member before he takes his seat.

The loyalty of Powell's Harlem constituency was legendary, but even their mood was changing as the 1960s came to an end. In the election of 1970, state assemblyman Charles Rangel defeated Powell in the Democratic primary election and went on to win the congressional seat that Powell had held for some twenty-four years.

Powell died two years later. His son by Yvette Diago, Adam Clayton Powell IV (he also had a son with Hazel Scott named Adam Clayton Powell III), later followed in his father's footsteps and represented East Harlem on the New York City Council. The portion of Seventh Avenue above 110th Street and a state office building in Harlem are named for Powell, and although he is not often included among the giants of civil rights, he made it possible for later generations of African American politicians, such as Jesse Jackson, to stand proud and unbowed in the political arena.

MAJOR GENERAL
BENJAMIN O.
DAVIS JR.

(B. 1912)

◆

The story of African Americans in the military in the twentieth century can be told almost completely through the career of one man: Benjamin O. Davis Jr. Like his father before him, he was a pioneer in the U.S. Army; but he would have even more success because of the changing times.

Davis was born on December 18, 1912, at just about the time his father, Benjamin O. Davis Sr., was assigned to service in the Mexican Border Patrol. Benjamin Jr. was only four years old when his mother, Elnora Dickerson Davis, died after giving birth to her third child. For a time, his father took care of the children with help from Elnora's sisters. But when Davis Sr. was posted to the Philippines, he sent the children to live with his parents in Washington, D.C. Three years later, Davis Sr. remarried, and the children went to live with him and their stepmother in Tuskegee, Alabama, where he taught military science and tactics at all-black Tuskegee Institute.

Benjamin Jr. was a typical "army brat." He moved often and learned early to adjust to new surroundings. He started public school at Tuskegee and finished in Cleveland, Ohio, at Central High School. In his senior year he was elected president of the student council.

Davis then enrolled at Western Reserve University but transferred to the University of Chicago, where he majored in mathematics. He made the move to Chicago because his father wanted him to go to the U.S. Military Academy at West Point. Chicago had a black congressman, Oscar De Priest, who would be able to appoint Davis to the academy. Davis was not so sure he wanted to follow in his father's footsteps, however. He had heard about the extreme prejudice at the academy. No black had graduated since Charles Young nearly fifty years before. And Davis knew firsthand about the segregation in the army, where his father had served in all-black units for his entire career. He did not approach the West Point entrance examination with enthusiasm. Still, it was a jolt when he learned that he had failed the test.

That failure was the spur that Davis needed. He determined he would prove—to his father and to himself—that he could not only qualify for the academy but do well. Reappointed by De Priest, he studied hard for the examination and passed. He entered West Point on July 1, 1923.

Resentful of someone different in their midst, the other cadets subjected Davis to the "silent treatment." For an entire year, no one spoke to him unless absolutely necessary. At the end of that plebe year, he was congratulated by some of his classmates, but the silence soon descended again. For his entire four years at West Point, he never had a roommate. But he did not complain—not even to his father. He realized that complaining would only make things worse, and that there was little he could do but stick it out and try to maintain his dignity as best he could.

At his graduation on June 12, 1936, Davis received his diploma from General John J. Pershing and his commission as a second lieutenant. He also received a rash of publicity as the first black West Point graduate in the twentieth century. That same year, he married Agatha Scott of New Haven, Connecticut, whom he had met in his junior year at the academy. The newlyweds traveled to Davis's first posting—Fort Benning, Georgia, in the heart of the segregated South.

Davis was promoted to first lieutenant in 1937, and two years later to captain. Every year, he was posted somewhere else. He worried that like his father he would be shuttled around as the army tried to find something for him to do that would not involve commanding white troops. But by the time he was promoted to captain, World War II would change everything.

In September 1939 Nazi forces under German leader Adolf Hitler invaded Poland and moved west, taking France in June 1940. England suffered under massive German bombing raids from August through October 1940. Many people in the United States were against entering the war to help England, but President Franklin D. Roosevelt believed that the country should be prepared for war. Not only was the Nazi threat real, but U.S. relations with Germany's ally Japan were deteriorating. It was time for action.

The Army Air Corps (there was no separate air force at the time) rushed to train more pilots. Pressured by black civil rights groups such as the National Association for the Advancement of Colored People (NAACP), the Army Air Corps established an Advanced Army Flying School at Tuskegee Institute. Benjamin O. Davis Jr. was in the first class of thirteen aviation cadets at Tuskegee.

On December 7, 1941, while Davis was at Tuskegee learning to fly, Japan bombed the U.S. Pacific Fleet at Pearl Harbor, Hawaii. After Pearl Harbor, there was no escape from the conflict that consumed the rest of the world. The United States entered World War II.

Davis was eager to get into the action, but the U.S. Army was not yet ready for a black flying squadron. Following graduation in the spring of 1942, Davis was appointed commandant of cadets at

LIEUTENANT COLONEL CHARITY ADAMS EARLEY (1918–2002)

The U.S. military was a leader in granting equal rights to black women as well as to black men. Charity Adams Earley was the commanding officer of the only organization of black women to serve overseas during World War II, the Central Postal Directory Battalion. When the battalion arrived in England in February 1945, Brigadier General Benjamin O. Davis, the highest-ranking black male commissioned officer, was there to greet them.

The battalion did not see combat. Instead, it broke all records for redirecting mail to and from all U.S. personnel in Europe—a total of seven million people, including Army, Navy, Marine Corps, civilians, and Red Cross workers. But Major Adams fought personal battles against segregated living quarters and recreational facilities and the racist general under whose command her battalion operated.

After the war ended, Adams chose not to remain in the military. Discharged in 1946 with the rank of lieutenant colonel, the highest rank below that of the Women's Army Corps (WAC) director, she earned degrees in psychology and put her knowledge to work in various jobs in personnel and teaching at the college level. She also got married and had two children.

In 1982, Earley was honored by the Smithsonian Institution in a salute to 110 of the most important women in black history. Seven years later, she published *One Woman's Army: A Black Officer Remembers the WAC*.

Tuskegee. He concentrated on excellence. He planned to be ready when the new U.S. Air Force allowed black fliers into the fight.

Finally, in early April 1943, the Ninety-ninth Pursuit Squadron, made up of airmen trained at Tuskegee and under the command of Colonel Benjamin O. Davis Jr., headed to North Africa, where Germany and its ally Italy were trying to gain control. On June 2, flying a strafing mission over an island off Sicily, the Ninety-ninth saw its first combat—but not the last. Early in July, the Ninety-ninth

Benjamin O. Davis Jr.'s 332d Fighter Group, the Tuskegee Airmen, listen for their orders.

invaded Sicily and helped to capture it. Afterward, Davis took charge of the 332d Fighter Group, which included three new squadrons and several support units. He returned to the United States, where a different kind of fight awaited him: attempts were being made to prevent black flying units from being assigned to combat areas. Davis testified forcefully to the competence and courage of his men. His persistence paid off.

In 1944, Davis's 332d finally headed out again for the Italian front. Soon joined by the Ninety-ninth Pursuit Squadron, the 332d was the largest fighter group there. They soon gained a reputation as skilled bomber escorts. It was deadly work. In October, a total of fifteen African American pilots were downed during their missions. The following April, after winter weather halted the air war, they flew fifty-four combat missions. They lost several planes and pilots but also shot down seventeen enemy aircraft.

Colonel Benjamin O. Davis Jr. stands at attention with his fellow officers as his father, Brigadier General Benjamin O. Davis Sr., pins the Distinguished Flying Cross on his uniform.

In April 1945, Germany surrendered; and in August, Japan surrendered. The war was over. General Benjamin O. Davis Sr. flew to Italy to personally pin the Distinguished Flying Cross on the uniform of his son, Colonel Benjamin O. Davis Jr.

Davis's next assignment was to head the 447th Bombardment Group, a newly trained black flying unit formed in 1943 under pressure from black groups and some members of Congress. The Air Force had no real intention of sending relatively inexperienced pilots on bombing missions and had hoped that the war would end before the 447th was sent into action. The war did end, and a new era was about to begin. President Roosevelt died in 1945, and his vice president, Harry S. Truman, assumed the presidency. In 1948, President Truman established a commission on equal treatment and opportunity for blacks in the armed services. Both General Davis and Colonel Davis testified before that commission that segregation was harmful not only to black servicemen but also to the armed services in general. The new Secretary of the Air Force, Stuart Symington, decided that

Colonel Davis's 332d would be the first all-black unit to be integrated into the larger air force.

Davis continued to receive promotions. Over the next two decades, he was named brigadier general (while serving in the Korean War in 1955) and later Chief of Staff, United Nations Command, the second highest position in the United Nations military. He became the first black to command an air base, Godman Field in Kentucky. He retired in 1970 at the age of fifty-seven, with the rank of permanent major general. In addition to the Distinguished Flying Cross, his medals included the Air Medal with four Oak Leaf Clusters, the Legion of Merit Award, and the French Croix de Guerre with Palm.

During General Davis's long career, blacks had managed to integrate just about all levels of the service, but Davis was "the only" or "the first" black in his positions and commands. In 1971, one year after his retirement, black officers still represented less than 2 percent of all the air force officers. But General Benjamin O. Davis Jr. was proud of his country's achievement. He entitled his autobiography *Benjamin O. Davis, Jr., American.*

ROSA
PARKS

(B . 1 9 1 3)

✦

There are some persistent myths about Rosa Parks, the woman who is often called the Mother of the Movement, and her role in the Montgomery bus boycott, which many feel signaled the start of the direct-action Civil Rights Movement. One is that she refused to give up her bus seat to a white passenger because she was tired after working all day as a department store seamstress. A related misunderstanding portrays her as old and largely innocent about what her refusal might mean. On the contrary, that evening in early December, Rosa Louise Parks was neither physically tired nor old. She was a healthy and active woman of forty-two and no more tired than usual after a day of work. She explains, "The only tired I was, was tired of giving in."[1]

Mrs. Parks was born in Tuskegee, Alabama, where Booker T. Washington had established Tuskegee Institute in 1881. Her father, James McCauley, was a carpenter, stonemason, and all-around builder, and her mother, Leona Edwards McCauley, was a teacher.

Rosa McCauley and her younger brother Sylvester were raised by their maternal grandparents in Pine Level, Alabama, while their mother was away teaching school during the week and their father traveled about building houses. The children grew up with a strong sense of what was fair and had a hard time accepting that living in the segregated South meant that, despite believing they were just as good as white people, they could not act as if they were.

Rosa McCauley attended school in Pine Level until she was eleven. Any black student who wanted to attend high school had to go to Montgomery, the closest city. Rosa lived with an aunt and attended a public junior high school for black students and later the laboratory school run by Alabama State Teachers' College for Negroes. Her schooling was interrupted when first her grandmother and then her mother became ill, and she went home to take care of them. She did not finish high school until after she was married.

She was nineteen years old when she married Raymond Parks, a barber ten years her senior. She was attracted to him for several reasons, one being that he was the first activist she had ever known. A member of the National Association for the Advancement of Colored People (NAACP), he often went to meetings or held them in his own home. By the early 1940s, the organization was trying to get more southern blacks to register to vote; and Rosa Parks decided to register. Blacks had to take a literacy test to ensure that they could read and write and understand the U.S. Constitution. The first two times Parks took the test, she was told she did not pass. Certain that she had, the third time she made a copy of her answers and told the registrar that she had done so. Realizing that Parks could prove she had passed, the registrar finally registered her.

Mrs. Parks joined the NAACP, only the second woman to join the Montgomery branch, and worked as its unpaid secretary. One of her duties was to keep records on cases of discrimination, unfair treatment, and violence against blacks. Usually, there was little the

NAACP could do. Witnesses were afraid to come forward and white authorities had no interest in fairness for blacks.

By the end of the 1940s, Mrs. Parks was also advising the NAACP Youth Council. She encouraged the young people to try to take out books from the main public library, rather than the colored library across town, but her project was unsuccessful. Still, there was reason for hope. The national NAACP had worked for years on school segregation cases in the courts, and when in May 1954 the U.S. Supreme Court declared "separate but equal" education unconstitutional, blacks across the nation had real hope for the future.

In the summer of 1955, Mrs. Parks attended a workshop at Highlander Folk School on a scholarship arranged by an influential white woman in Montgomery, Mrs. Virginia Durr. At the school, located in Monteagle, Tennessee, Mrs. Parks participated in workshops in school desegregation and enjoyed the rare experience of meeting and living in peace and harmony with whites. All too soon, she had to return to the segregation of Montgomery.

One of the most galling aspects of life under segregation were the bus segregation laws and customs. Blacks were 66 percent of the ridership, but they had to pay at the front and then enter at the back, sit in the back of the bus, and even give up their seats if the seats reserved for whites were filled. Montgomery NAACP members had spoken about challenging bus segregation in the courts and were looking for the right case—one featuring a woman of good reputation. As the organization's secretary, Mrs. Parks had participated in these discussions; but her own bus incident was not planned—either by the NAACP or by herself. She was just sick of the unfair treatment.

Arrested for refusing to give up her bus seat to a white person, she became a symbol for Montgomery's blacks. Urged on by Jo Ann Robinson, a professor of English at Alabama State College, and by local black ministers, the majority refused to ride the segregated city buses. Martin Luther King Jr., the young minister of the Dexter

Avenue Baptist Church, rose to leadership of the Montgomery bus boycott, inspiring the city's blacks to stay off the buses and raising funds to buy vans operated by the churches to take the people to work.

The boycott lasted more than a year and did not end until the U.S. Supreme Court ruled that segregation on public transportation was unconstitutional. It inspired other southern blacks to engage in direct action and nonviolent efforts to achieve their rights as citizens and is generally considered the spark to the movement.

Mrs. Rosa Parks left Montgomery soon after the boycott ended. Her family was besieged with threatening telephone calls. She could

DAISY BATES (1914–1999)

Born one year after Rosa Parks, Daisy Gatson Bates made her own mark on civil rights history two years after Parks made her courageous stand on a Montgomery, Alabama, bus. In 1957, Bates, who was president of the Arkansas NAACP, led the fight to admit nine black students to Central High School in Little Rock, Arkansas. She nurtured the students, encouraged them to be brave, and tried to guard them against howling white mobs. Rocks were thrown through her window and a burning cross was placed on her roof; but she and the students persevered. After Arkansas governor Orval Faubus sent state National Guardsmen to Little Rock to prevent the students from enrolling at the school, President Dwight D. Eisenhower had no choice but to send U.S. troops to enforce the 1954 Supreme Court decision to outlaw racial segregation in schools. The Little Rock school desegregation victory was one of the major early successes of the civil rights movement.

The newspaper published by Bates and her husband, L.C. Bates, was ultimately destroyed financially as a result of her campaign. The couple left Arkansas. While he served with the NAACP, she wrote a book about her experiences, which was published in 1962. The following year, she was the only woman who spoke at the March on Washington.

not find a job. The family moved to Detroit, Michigan, where Rosa's brother Sylvester lived.

During the bus boycott and for several years afterward, Mrs. Parks often traveled around the country giving speeches and accepting honors for her part in sparking the civil rights movement. But she played no official role. Women were kept in the background. At the 1963 March on Washington, she was part of a group of wives of major civil rights organization leaders and other important women who marched separately. At a special Tribute to Women during the ceremonies, A. Philip Randolph introduced her and other women who had participated in the struggle. But she was not asked to speak. "Nowadays," Mrs. Parks told this writer in 1990, "women wouldn't stand for being kept so much in the background, but back then women's rights hadn't become a popular cause yet."[2]

For many years after that, Mrs. Parks lived quietly in Detroit, working in the office of Michigan Congressman John Conyers and caring for her mother, brother, and husband. All three loved ones died in the late 1970s. In 1987, she formed the Rosa and Raymond Parks Institute for Self-Development, whose purpose was to help youth continue their education and have hope for the future. Raising funds for the institute became easier as more and more organizations sought to honor her for her role in bringing about equal rights for her people. She has received countless honorary degrees from colleges and other honors.

Cleveland Avenue in Montgomery was renamed for her, as was Twelfth Street in Detroit. A bust of Mrs. Parks was unveiled at the Smithsonian Institution in 1991. In 1996, President Bill Clinton presented her with the Presidential Medal of Freedom, and in 1999 she accepted the Congressional Gold Medal.

ROBINSON

✦

Jackie Robinson, the man who broke the racial barrier in American sports, was born in Cairo, Georgia, a year after World War I ended. Six months after his birth, his father, Jerry Robinson, deserted the family, and not long after that his mother, Mallie, took her five children to California seeking a better life. They rode in a segregated railroad car to Pasadena, where they settled in a working-class neighborhood. Mallie worked as a domestic, and the children took care of each other.

Eventually, Mallie managed to buy a small house in a predominantly white neighborhood. Their white neighbors on Pepper Street tried to get them out, shouting curses, signing petitions, and offering to buy the house. But Mallie Robinson insisted that her family had a right to live wherever they wished, and the Robinson family stayed put.

All the Robinson children were fine athletes, but Jackie was the strongest competitor. At John Muir Technical High School, Robinson won letters in track, football, basketball, and baseball. But unlike the white players on his teams, he received no college scholarship offers. He so excelled at Pasadena Junior College, however, that senior colleges

took notice. He attended the University of California at Los Angeles (UCLA) on scholarship and became UCLA's first four-letter man.

Robinson dropped out of UCLA when he was just a few credits shy of graduation. His mother, who had worked so hard to support her family, was at the point of collapse, and he got a job to take care of her. But soon he, like legions of other young American men, was in the military. On December 7, 1941, Japanese planes had bombed the U.S. naval base at Pearl Harbor in Hawaii, and the United States was thrust into World War II.

On his discharge from the army in 1945, Robinson signed with the Kansas City Monarchs, a Negro League baseball team. Just as there were National and American Leagues in white baseball, so there were National and American Leagues in Negro baseball. But there the similarities ended. Negro League players earned comparatively low wages and worked under poor conditions. But their talent was unmistakable. Branch Rickey, owner of the Brooklyn Dodgers, decided that it was time to break the color barrier in professional baseball. For three years, his scouts had been searching for a highly talented young black player. It did not take long for them to find Jackie Robinson. In August 1945, as his first season with the Monarchs came to an end, Robinson met with Rickey.

The first black player in white baseball would have to be more than a great baseball player. He would have to have the courage to withstand a barrage of publicity and prejudice. In order to underscore the necessity of forbearance, Ricky compared what was in store for Robinson to what Jesus Christ suffered. Robinson decided he could do it. He signed with the Dodgers' farm team in Montreal and played there for two years before joining the main team.

Robinson married Rachel Isman, whom he had met when both were at UCLA, and their first child was born in early 1947. Just a few months later, on April 15, 1947, opening day of baseball season, Robinson took his position at first base at Brooklyn's Ebbets Field. He had already survived a petition drive on the part of some of his team-mates to keep him off the team, and there was much more to come. Pitchers deliberately tried to hit him with the ball, base runners dug the spikes of their shoes into his shins, opposing players on the bench shouted epithets, and fans mocked him from the stands and sent death threats. But he carried himself with dignity, refused to respond in kind, and played the best baseball he could. In 1949, he was voted the Most Valuable Player of the American League, leading the league with a .342 average and thirty-two steals. He also had career highs in runs batted in (RBIs) with 124 and 122 runs.

Robinson, having proved himself as a baseball player that season, came into his own as a man. He now felt free to speak his mind—to his teammates, opposition teams, umpires, and anyone else.

During that season, the great African American singer and human rights activist Paul Robeson made a remark in a speech in Paris that caused an uproar. He said, in effect, that it would be "unthinkable" for black Americans to fight in a war against Russia because blacks were treated better in Russia than they were in the United States. This statement upset many in the U.S. Congress. In fact, the House Un-American Activities Committee (HUAC) convened hearings on the incident, to which they called prominent African Americans to testify about Robeson's statement. The first person called was Jackie Robinson. Robinson was not eager to testify, but he knew that he could not refuse to do so without risking his athletic career. So he turned his appearance before the committee into an opportunity. In his testimony on July 14, 1949, he said he thought Robeson's statement, if accurately quoted, was silly. But he understood the sentiments behind it. He spent most of his time before the committee condemning racism in America. Other witnesses did the same, and HUAC took no further action.

Robinson often used his fame as a platform to speak out against racism. Many sportswriters grumbled that he should stick to sports, but Robinson realized he had opportunities enjoyed by few other black Americans.

In December 1956, after a decade with the Brooklyn Dodgers, Robinson was traded to the New York Giants. But he chose not to remain in baseball. A month later, he announced his retirement. He served as a vice president for Chock Full o' Nuts for a time, then opened his own construction company. He became active in the National Association for the Advancement of Colored People (NAACP) and often served as a main speaker at fundraisers and rallies. He received the NAACP's Spingarn Medal in 1956 for meritorious service to black America. He also served as chairman of the Freedom Fund Drive, which sought to raise $1 million for Thurgood Marshall and the NAACP Legal Defense Fund.

He sadly watched as younger African Americans became more militant and put aside nonviolent efforts to achieve equality. In a letter to a special assistant to President Richard M. Nixon in the spring of 1972, he wrote: "Black America has asked so little, but if you can't see the anger that comes from rejection, you are treading a dangerous course. We older blacks, unfortunately, were willing to wait. Today's young blacks are ready to explode! We had better take some definitive action or I am afraid the consequences could be nation shattering. I hope you are willing to listen to the cries of the black youth. We cannot afford additional conflict."[1]

By the time he wrote this letter, Robinson was suffering from diabetes and heart disease. He died of a heart attack six months later, at the age of fifty-three. In the years that followed, he would be honored and remembered often as the man who broke the color barrier in major league baseball. But his widow, Rachel Robinson, liked to remind people that he was more than that: "In remembering him," she once said, "I tend to de-emphasize him as a ball player and emphasize him as an informal civil rights leader. That's the part that drops out, that people forget."[2]

WHITNEY M.
YOUNG JR.
(1921–1971)

◆

While Jackie Robinson was an "unofficial" civil rights leader, as his widow Rachel put it, Whitney M. Young Jr. was officially so. As head of the National Urban League, he was one of the half-dozen civil rights leaders who were known as the Big Six. Less well known than men like A. Philip Randolph and Martin Luther King Jr., Young was nevertheless a highly influential leader who was an effective behind-the-scenes negotiator.

Whitney Moore Young Jr. was born on the campus of Lincoln Institute in Lincoln Ridge, Kentucky, where his father was president. Young's mother, Laura Ray Young, was the first African American postmaster in Kentucky and the second in the United States.

Young graduated from Lincoln Institute as valedictorian of his class and then enrolled in the pre-med program at Kentucky State Industrial, another historically black institution. Having grown up among the educated black elite of the South, he planned a career as a doctor, one of the most respected professions in the black community. But after a year of pre-medical studies, he changed his mind. He

99

dropped out of college and taught at a nearby school for a year before he joined the army.

The United States was in the midst of World War II, and the U.S. military was segregated. The majority of black soldiers were assigned to construction, kitchen, and other noncombat duties under the supervision of white officers. Young soon distinguished himself as a mediator between his unit's white captain and the black troops, and found the experience of defusing racial tensions so gratifying that he decided to pursue a career in race relations after the war.

After his discharge from the army, Young returned to Kentucky State Industrial College. He married Margaret Buckner in 1944, and the couple had two daughters. Young earned his bachelor's degree from the college in 1946 and then enrolled at the University of Minnesota, earning his master's degree in social work in 1947.

While in St. Paul, Minnesota, Young joined the local chapter of the National Urban League. The organization, founded in 1910, just one year after the formation of the National Association for the Advancement of Colored People (NAACP), was also an interracial organization. Its stated purpose was to further the economic progress of blacks, especially in the cities, as its name suggests. Young worked his way up in the ranks of the organization, serving as executive secretary of the Omaha, Nebraska, branch of the league while teaching social work at the University of Nebraska and Creighton University.

In 1954, Young accepted the position of dean of the Atlanta University School of Social Work. He joined the Atlanta branch of the Urban League and also the Atlanta Council on Human Relations. Blacks in the cities of the South were chafing under the rigid rules of segregation, and in the year following Young's return to the South that unrest coalesced around the arrest of Rosa Parks for challenging the segregation of that city's buses. In Atlanta, as co-chairman of the Atlanta Council on Human Relations, Young helped to desegregate the city's public library system.

In 1961, at the age of forty, Young became president of the National Urban League and moved to the organization's headquarters in New York City. At the time, the league seemed to have lost its sense of purpose and had taken a backseat to more activist organizations, such as the Congress of Racial Equality (CORE) (formed in 1942) and the Southern Christian Leadership Conference (SCLC) (established by Martin Luther King Jr. and other southern ministers after the successful Montgomery, Alabama, bus boycott). Young launched what he called Operation Rescue to revitalize the organization and turn it into an aggressive fighter for civil rights and justice. He expanded its staff

JAMES FARMER (1914–1999)

Born in Marshall, Texas, James Farmer, like Young, was the son of a college professor. He earned a divinity degree from Howard University but was never ordained as a Methodist minister. He decided he would rather fight the church's segregated policies than uphold them. In 1942, while doing further graduate work at the University of Chicago, he and a group of fellow students founded the Congress of Racial Equality (CORE), the first black organization to use the techniques of nonviolent protest and passive resistance. CORE pioneered the sit-in to integrate a local restaurant in 1943. More willing to confront the white power structure than the NAACP or the Urban League, CORE also started the Freedom Rides in 1961.

By the late 1960s, CORE had taken a militant stance that Farmer could not support. He left the organization and ran for Congress on the Republican Party ticket but was defeated by the Democrat Shirley Chisholm. Not long afterward, he joined the administration of Republican President Richard Nixon as assistant secretary of health, education, and welfare. He is credited with coining the term "affirmative action." Retiring from politics in 1971, Farmer spent the rest of his life lecturing and writing. In 1998, the year before he died, President Bill Clinton awarded him the Presidential Medal of Freedom.

from 38 to 1,600 and its annual budget of $325,000 to more than $6 million. When members of the organization's board were reluctant to support A. Philip Randolph's March on Washington in 1963, fearing that it was too radical, Young persuaded them that the league's influence would actually serve to balance and neutralize the radical elements.

More militant African Americans sometimes charged that Young was too conservative and too passive with whites. He was a mediator who preferred reason and persuasion to direct challenges. He was quietly successful in persuading major corporations to hire more blacks and to support job training initiatives in the cities. During the administration of President Lyndon B. Johnson, Young devised what he called a "Domestic Marshall Plan." It was modeled on the efforts of the United States to help Europe recover after the devastation of World War II and sought to increase spending on education and vocational training, housing, and health services. Johnson later incorporated elements of Young's plan into his own War on Poverty. In 1968, Johnson recognized Young's service to the nation by awarding him the Presidential Medal of Freedom.

Young, who published two books and many articles and speeches, once wrote, "You can holler, protest, march, picket and demonstrate, but somebody must be able to sit in on the strategy conferences and plot a course. There must be strategists, the researchers, the professionals to carry out the program. That's our role."[1]

In March 1971, Young traveled to Lagos, Nigeria, to attend a conference of black leaders. On March 11 he relaxed by going for a swim and suffered a fatal heart attack. He was forty-nine years old.

Young's birthplace is now a National Historic Landmark, and the campus of the former Kentucky Institute is the Whitney M. Young Jr. Job Training Corps Center.

KING Jr.

(1929–1968)

✦

Martin Luther King Jr., the man who is most strongly associated with the nonviolent campaign for civil rights in the United States, was born in 1929. The Stock Market crashed that year, and the Great Depression soon followed. The King family did not suffer as much as most black Americans from the effects of the Depression. The Reverend Martin Luther King Sr. was pastor of Ebenezer Baptist Church, and his wife, Alberta Williams King, was a schoolteacher, one of the few professions open to black women at that time. No matter how bad the economy, churches still needed pastors and schools still needed teachers.

Martin Jr., his older sister Christine, and his younger brother Arthur were raised in comfort, but their parents could not shield them from the racism that was all around them. The best the elder Kings could do was teach their children that they were as good as anyone else and that, while they might have to live with segregation, they did not have to bow to it. One time Martin was riding in the car with his father when a police officer stopped them. Like most white

southerners, the officer called the elder King "Boy." The Reverend King pointed to his son and said, "This is a boy. I am a man, and until you call me one, I will not listen to you."[1]

Martin Luther King Jr. felt a powerful inner urge to help his fellow man, and by the time he was a senior in high school he decided to become a minister like his father. While attending a seminary school in Pennsylvania, he heard a lecture about Mohandas K. Gandhi, who had brought about India's independence from Great Britain through nonviolent protest. The notion of bringing about revolutionary change by nonviolent means excited Martin, and he read all he could about Gandhi's tactics. He could not, however, imagine how those methods could be used against segregation in the American South. The efforts of British authorities to arrest and imprison Gandhi and his followers paled in comparison to the long history of southern white brutality against blacks who sought to question their second-class status.

After graduating from seminary school, King enrolled in the doctor of theology program at Boston University. He met and married Coretta Scott, a student at the New England Conservatory of Music in Boston and a native of Alabama. When the Dexter Avenue Baptist Church in Montgomery, Alabama, invited him to be its pastor, the young couple returned to the South.

The Kings arrived in Montgomery in September 1954. Just a few months earlier, in May, the U.S. Supreme Court had ruled that segregated schools were unconstitutional. Although the Kings hoped that segregation would be ended in other areas of life as well, they held out little hope of anything happening soon in Montgomery, which was rigidly segregated.

Then, fourteen months later, all that changed. Mrs. Rosa Parks was arrested for refusing to give up her seat on a segregated city bus. Jo Ann Robinson, a professor of English at Alabama State College, organized a one-day boycott of the buses. Montgomery's black leaders met and decided to continue the protest. They formed the

Montgomery Improvement Association and elected as its president the young new pastor of Dexter Avenue Baptist Church. They did not know much about him, but they did know that he was so new in town that he had not had time to make any strong friends or enemies. He had not accepted favors from the whites of Montgomery and so did not owe them anything.

King was astonished to be elected. But he realized this was an opportunity to preach the kind of nonviolent activism that Gandhi had used in India. In his very first speech without prepared notes, he set the tone for the nonviolent, direct-action Civil Rights Movement that would change America.

The Montgomery bus boycott was long and hard and frequently met with harsh and repressive tactics on the part of the city's whites. But the people's determination not to suffer the humiliation of segregation in Montgomery any longer, and King's inspiring leadership, brought about the change they had sought.

After the boycott ended, King decided to build upon that success. He formed a new organization of southern black ministers called the Southern Christian Leadership Conference (SCLC). Since older civil rights organizations like the National Association for the Advancement of Colored People (NAACP), the National Urban League, and the Congress of Racial Equality (CORE) were already fighting discrimination and segregation, the SCLC chose to focus on voting rights. But the SCLC was unable to inspire the same excitement with its voting rights campaign as the bus boycott had enjoyed.

Then, in early 1960, black southern college students took the fight against segregation into their own hands. Supported by CORE, they revived the tactic of sitting in (which was introduced by CORE back in the early 1940s) at segregated lunch counters. The movement spread like wildfire, and King decided to organize the students. The Student Nonviolent Coordinating Committee (SNCC) was born. The students engaged in the tactics of confrontation, and although King worried about them, he had to admit they were effective. While working behind the scenes to negotiate with authorities, he publicly supported the students' tactics.

White response became increasingly violent. In Albany, Georgia, and Birmingham, Alabama, police beat, arrested, and jailed hundreds of protesters. Ordinary citizens and white supremacist groups attacked and killed civil rights workers, bombed a church in Birmingham, and threatened the lives and bombed the homes of civil rights leaders like King. But southern blacks, now often joined by northern college students and ministers, both white and black, kept on.

At the March on Washington for Jobs and Freedom in August 1963, King made the most stirring public speech of his career—and of the Civil Rights Movement. In his "I have a dream" speech, he gave voice to the yearnings of an entire people. He emerged from that march as the premier civil rights leader in the country. In 1964, he was awarded the Nobel Prize for Peace, only the second African American to be so honored. The prize, given by the Norwegian Parliament, is the highest international honor.

After the U.S. government passed the Civil Rights Act of 1964 and the Voting Rights Act of 1965, the task of the direct-action Civil Rights Movement was over, but that did not mean that discrimination had ended in America. King realized that northern blacks had hardly been touched by the movement. They were not legally segregated, but they faced severe discrimination in housing, education, and employment. King tried to take the movement to the northern cities, but he failed to capture the imagination of urban blacks. Many younger African Americans believed that the terror and horrible violence suffered by civil rights workers in the South was too big a price to pay and that the time for nonviolence was over. SNCC changed its name to the Student National Coordinating Committee and began to advocate "Black Power!" The Black Panthers and the Nation of Islam, also known as the Black Muslims, preached black separatism and self-determination, not integration and nonviolence.

Martin Luther King Jr. was an internationally recognized leader who had lost his platform. He looked for another cause and decided to speak for the poor and downtrodden. He was in the midst of planning, with others in the SCLC, a Poor People's March on Washington in the spring of 1968 when he responded to a request to go to Memphis, Tennessee, to show his support of striking black sanitation workers. There, in Memphis, he was struck down by an assassin's bullet in the prime of his life. He was not yet forty years old.

Martin Luther King was a singular leader at a unique time in American history. In 1984, in recognition of his contribution to his country, his birthday was made a national holiday.

CHRONOLOGY

1850	Of the nearly 400,000 free blacks in the United States, 3,000 own land
1856	Booker T. Washington born
	Lieutenant Henry O. Flipper born
1857	In the case of *Scott* v. *Sanford*, the U.S. Supreme Court rules against citizenship for blacks
1861	Civil War begins
1862	Ida B. Wells-Barnett born
1863	Emancipation Proclamation issued by President Abraham Lincoln frees all slaves in the Confederate States
	Fifty-fourth Massachusetts Volunteer Regiment mustered into service and assaults Fort Wagner, South Carolina
1865	Civil War ends
	President Lincoln assassinated
	Congress passes the Thirteenth Amendment, abolishing slavery in the United States; it is later ratified
1866	Congress passes the first Civil Rights Act declaring free blacks to be U.S. citizens
1867	Congress passes the first Reconstruction Act, requiring former Confederate states to ratify the "Civil War Amendments," write new constitutions, and grant voting rights to all men, regardless of "race, color, or previous condition of servitude"
	Howard University founded in Washington, D.C.
1868	Congress passes the Fourteenth Amendment, granting blacks full citizenship and equal civil rights
	W. E. B. Du Bois born
1870	The Fifteenth Amendment to the U.S. Constitution guarantees the right to vote to all men, regardless of color
1875	Mary McLeod Bethune born
	Carter G. Woodson born
1877	Reconstruction ends
1881	Booker T. Washington founds Tuskegee Institute in Alabama
1887	Marcus Garvey born
1889	A. Philip Randolph born

1896	In the case of *Plessy* v. *Ferguson,* the U.S. Supreme Court rules that "separate but equal" facilities for blacks are constitutional
1898	Spanish-American War
	Paul Robeson born
1901	Louis "Satchmo" Armstrong born
1904	Mary McLeod Bethune opens her school, which merges with Cookman College in 1922 to become Bethune-Cookman College
1908	Thurgood Marshall born
	Adam Clayton Powell Jr. born
1909	National Association for the Advancement of Colored People (NAACP) founded
	William Edward Burghardt Du Bois becomes editor of *The Crisis* magazine
1912	Major General Benjamin O. Davis, Jr. born
1913	Rosa Parks born
1914	World War I begins in Europe
1915	Booker T. Washington dies
1917	United States enters World War I
1918	World War I ends
1919	Jackie Robinson born
1921	Whitney M. Young Jr. born
1929	Stock Market crash ushers in the Great Depression
	Martin Luther King Jr. born
1939	World War II begins in Europe
1940	Lieutenant Henry O. Flipper dies
	Marcus Garvey dies
1941	United States enters World War II
	The Great Depression ends
1945	World War II ends
1950	Carter G. Woodson dies
1953	Korean War ends
1954	In the case of *Brown* v. *Board of Education of Topeka,* the U.S. Supreme Court rules that "separate but equal" schools are unconstitutional and orders integration "with all deliberate speed"

1955	Mary McCleod Bethune dies
1961	America enters the Vietnam War
1963	Martin Luther King Jr. tells the March on Washington, "I have a dream"
	W. E. B. Du Bois dies
1964	Congress passes a Civil Rights Act, enforcing the right to vote and outlawing discrimination in public accommodation, education, and employment
1965	Congress passes the Voting Rights Act to enforce the Fifteenth Amendment and guaranteeing the right to vote of all citizens
1968	Martin Luther King Jr. dies
1971	A. Philip Randolph dies
	Louis "Satchmo" Armstrong dies
	Whitney M. Young Jr. dies
1972	Adam Clayton Powell Jr. dies
	Jackie Robinson dies
1976	Paul Robeson dies
1993	Thurgood Marshall dies

NOTES

BOOKER T. WASHINGTON

1. William E. B. DuBois, James Weldon Johnson, and Booker T. Washington, *Three Negro Classics* (New York: Avon Books, 1965), 44–45.
2. Ibid., 51.
3. Ibid., 68.
4. Ibid., 87.
5. Ibid., 108.
6. Ibid., 149.
7. Ibid., 252.

LIEUTENANT HENRY O. FLIPPER

1. John M. Carroll, *The Black Military Experience in the American West* (New York: Liveright Publishing, 1971), 348–349.

CARTER G. WOODSON

1. "The Unfinished Business of Carter G. Woodson," *City Sun* (March 20–26, 1991), 31.
2. Anna Rothe, ed., *Current Biography 1944* (New York: H. W. Wilson Company, 1944), 743.

MARY MCLEOD BETHUNE

1. Gerda Lerner, ed., *Black Women in White America: A Documentary History* (New York: Vintage Books, 1973), 135.
2. Ibid., 136.
3. Ibid.
4. Ibid.
5. Ibid., 137.
6. Ibid.
7. Ibid., 139.
8. Madeline Stratton, *Negroes Who Helped Build America* (Boston: Ginn and Company, 1965), 82.
9. Ibid.
10. Lerner, *Black Women in White America*, 142.
11. Stratton, *Negroes Who Helped Build America*, 87.
12. "My Last Will and Testament," *Ebony* (November 1973), 84–86.

W. E. B. DuBOIS

1. Walter Wilson, ed., *The Selected Writings of W. E. B. DuBois* (New York: A Mentor Book, 1970), 255.
2. Lerone Bennett Jr., *Pioneers in Protest* (Chicago: Johnson Publishing Company Inc., 1968), 246.
3. Ibid., 248.
4. Ibid., 242.
5. Rayford W. Logan and Michael R. Winston, eds., *Dictionary of American Negro Biography* (New York: W. W. Norton & Company, 1982), 195.
6. Bennett, Pioneers in Protest, 249.
7. Ibid., 250–251.

8. Wilson, *Selected Writings of W. E. B. DuBois*, 102–103.

9. Logan and Winston, *Dictionary of American Negro Biography*, 198.

MARCUS GARVEY

1. "Marcus Garvey: Look for Me in the Whirlwind," PBS, *The American Experience*, www.pbs.org/wgbh/amex/garvey/.

PAUL ROBESON

1. Carlyle Douglas, "Farewell to a Fighter," *Ebony* (April 1976), 34.

2. Ibid.

3. Alden Whitman, "Paul Robeson Dead at 77, Singer, Actor and Activist," *New York Times*, January 24, 1976, 125, no. 43, 099, 1; as cited in the *New York Times*, January 24, 1976, 125, no. 43, 099, 1; as cited in the *New York Times Obituaries Index*, 1969-1978 (New York: The New York Times Company, 1980), 162.

LOUIS "SATCHMO" ARMSTRONG

1. Gary Giddins, *Satchmo* (1998; reprint, New York: Da Capo Press, 1998), 48.

2. Louis Armstrong, *Satchmo: My Life in New Orleans* (1954; reprint, New York: Da Capo Press, 1986), 28.

3. Ibid., 51.

4. Giddins, 165.

THURGOOD MARSHALL

1. James Haskins, *Thurgood Marshall: A Life for Justice* (New York: Henry Holt & Co., 1992), 93.

2. The Oyez Project, Northwestern University: http://oyez.nwu.edu/justices/justices.cgi?justice_id=96&page=biography.

ADAM CLAYTON POWELL JR.

1. James Haskins, *Adam Clayton Powell: Portrait of a Marching Black* (New York: Dial Press, 1974), 122.

ROSA PARKS

1. Rosa Parks, with Jim Haskins, *Rosa Parks: My Story* (New York: Dial Press, 1992), 116.

2. Ibid., 165.

JACKIE ROBINSON

1. National Archives and Records Administration, *Jackie Robinson: Civil Rights Advocate*, www.nara.gov/education/teaching/robinson/robmain.html.

2. Ibid.

WHITNEY M. YOUNG JR.

1. Rudi Williams, "Whitney M. Young Jr.: Little Known Civil Rights Pioneer," American Forces Information Services, www.defenselink.mil/news/Feb2002/n02012002_200202011.html.

MARTIN LUTHER KING JR.

1. James Haskins, *The Life and Death of Martin Luther King, Jr.* (New York: Lothrop, Lee & Shepard Co., 1977), 16.

BIBLIOGRAPHY

Dickerson, Dennis C. *Militant Mediator: Whitney M. Young, Jr.* Lexington, KY: The University Press of Kentucky, 1998.

Frommer, Harvey. *Jackie Robinson.* New York: Franklin Watts, 1984.

Haskins, James. *Adam Clayton Powell, Jr.: Portrait of a Marching Black.* New York: Dial Press, 1974.

————. *Bayard Rustin: Behind the Scenes of the Civil Rights Movement.* New York: Hyperion Books for Children, 1997.

————. *Profiles in Black Power.* New York: Doubleday, 1972.

————. *The March on Washington.* New York: HarperCollins Publishers, 1993.

————. *Thurgood Marshall: A Life for Justice.* New York: Henry Holt & Co., 1992, p. 93.

McKissack, Patricia, and Fredrick McKissack. *A Long Hard Journey: The Story of the Pullman Porter.* New York: Walker & Co., 1989.

"Marcus Garvey: Look for Me in the Whirlwind," PBS' *The American Experience.* www.pbs.org/wgbh/amex/garvey/

Parks, Rosa, with Jim Haskins. *Rosa Parks: My Story.* New York: Dial Press, 1992.

Washington, James M., Jr., Ed. *A Testament of Hope: The Essential Writings and Speeches of Martin Luther King, Jr.* San Francisco, CA: HarperCollins Publishers, 1986.

PICTURE CREDITS

AUTHOR CREDITS

KEY:

Military Heroes: Jim Haskins, *African American Military Heroes* (New York: John Wiley & Sons, Inc., 1998).

Musicians: Eleanora Tate, *African American Musicians* (New York: John Wiley & Sons, Inc., 2000).

Teachers: Clinton Cox, *African American Teachers* (New York: John Wiley & Sons, Inc., 2000).

Writers: Brenda Wilkinson, *African American Women Writers* (New York: John Wiley & Sons, Inc., 2000).

BY JIM HASKINS
Lieutenant Henry O. Flipper, Major General Benjamin O. Davis Jr: adapted from *Military Heroes*. Marcus Garvey, A. Philip Randolph, Thurgood Marshall, Adam Clayton Powell Jr., Rosa Parks, Jackie Robinson, Whitney M. Young Jr., Martin Luther King Jr.

BY CLINTON COX
Booker T. Washington, Carter G. Woodson, Mary McLeod Bethune, W. E. B. Du Bois: adapted from *Teachers*.

BY ELEANORA TATE
Paul Robeson, Louis "Satchmo" Armstrong: adapted from *Musicians*.

BY BRENDA WILKINSON
Ida B. Wells-Barnett: adapted from *Writers*.

INDEX